of Trento, Italy.

D1331472

000002007081

THE BASICS

THE QUR'AN

THE BASICS

SECOND EDITION

Massimo Campanini

Translated from the Italian by Oliver Leaman

Routledge
Taylor & Francis Group

NEW YORK AND LONDON

Second edition published 2016
by Routledge
711 Third Avenue, New York, NY 10017

and by Routledge
2 Park Square, Milton Park, Abingdon, Oxon, OX14 4RN

Routledge is an imprint of the Taylor & Francis Group, an informa business

© 2016 Taylor & Francis

First edition published by Routledge 2007

Library of Congress Cataloging-in-Publication Data
Names: Campanini, Massimo, 1954– , author. | Leaman, Oliver, 1950–, translator.
Title: The Qur'an: the basics / Massimo Campanini ; translated from the Italian
    by Oliver Leaman.
Other titles: Corano e la sua interpretazione. English
Description: Second edition. | New York, NY: Routledge, 2016. |
    Series: The basics | Includes bibliographical references.
Identifiers: LCCN 2015048635 | ISBN 9781138666306 (hbk)
Subjects: LCSH: Qur'an—Criticism, interpretation, etc.
Classification: LCC BP130.1 .C3613 2016 | DDC 297.1/2261—dc23
LC record available at http://lccn.loc.gov/2015048635

ISBN: 978-1-138-66630-6 (hbk)
ISBN: 978-1-138-66631-3 (pbk)
ISBN: 978-1-315-61945-3 (ebk)

Typeset in Bembo and Scala Sans
by Apex CoVantage, LLC
Printed in Great Britain by Ashford Colour Press Ltd

CONTENTS

1

ISLAM AND THE QUR'AN

The Qur'an is the sacred book of Islam. In Islamic culture it is the Book. It represents a point of essential reference to the essence of Islamic culture and is referred to on a daily basis by believers primarily as a religious guide but also in everyday colloquial expressions. In order to understand in what sense and how the Qur'an carries out these functions, it is necessary to discuss the nature of Islam itself.

WHAT IS ISLAM?

Islam is of course a religion. That seems to be an obvious, even banal, remark. But it is important to establish that using the word religion to define Islam is, if not a mistake, at least rather imprecise. It is worth noting that from a methodological perspective terms like "religion" or "theology" are problematic or ambiguous, especially when applied to Islam. We will not make progress if we seek to define an expression such as the Islamic religion as though it is like the Christian religion. Similarly, theology in Islam is not the study of God, or argument about God, despite the literal sense of the Greek word (*theos*, "God"; *logos*, "reasoning"), but takes on an apologetic and dialectic character, as compared with dealing with divine issues.

In Arabic the word "religion" when applied to Islam may be translated in a number of ways, but the most satisfactory and precise term for it is *din*. The Qur'an states at least twice that Islam is "the" *din*. For example, at 5.3: "Today I have perfected your religion (*din*) for you. I have applied my favor to you and have chosen Islam for you as your religion (*din*)" (but see also 3.19). In the context, however, the term Islam cannot refer to a "historical" Islam ("Islamdom", Marshall Hodgson would have said), which did not yet exist. At the time of the Prophet neither an Islamic state nor an Islamic nation or empire existed. Islamic theology and philosophy did not exist as well; no "dogma" was established, no jurisprudence codified. Thus "Islam" must be understood as the "natural", "monotheistic" religion wherein all humans are born. This natural inclination to God, this "submission" to God's will, is truly "Islam".

Secondly, a widely accepted definition contains three things: *iman*, *ihsan* and *islam*—that is, faith, right behavior and submission. Faith leads, right behavior binds and submission implies future retribution. A famous *hadith*—a reporting of a saying or an action of the Prophet Muhammad, transmitted among others by al-Nawawi—consists of the following anecdote:

> One day, while we were sitting down listening to the Messenger of God, a man appeared in white clothes and with dark black hair. He did not look as though he had been on a journey and none of us knew who he was. He sat in front of the Prophet, put his knees together and the palms of his hands on his thighs, and said "Oh Muhammad, tell me what *Islam* is". The Messenger of God said "Islam is that you bear witness that there is no other God than God and that Muhammad is the Messenger of God, that you carry out the ritual prayer, give *zakat* [alms], fast in the month of Ramadan and make pilgrimage to the House [the sacred mosque in Mecca], if you can". "You say the truth", the man said. We were surprised that he had been able to question the Prophet and been answered. The man then asked "Tell me what *iman* [faith] is". The Prophet replied "It is that you believe in God, in his angels, in his Books, in his Messengers, and in the Last Day, and that you believe in the divine decree, and that it determines the good and the bad". "You said the truth" replied the man, asking again "Tell me what is *ihsan* [right conduct]". He replied "It is that you love God as though you see him, for if you do not see Him, He certainly sees you". The man said "Tell me what the Hour [of final judgment] is". The Prophet replied "He who is questioned does not know any more than he who asked the question". [. . .] After that the man disappeared

and only I remained. Then the Prophet asked me "Omar, do you know who that was who questioned me?" I replied "God and His Messenger will surely know more about it". "It was Gabriel" he said "who came to teach you your religion".

(al-Nawawi 1990: 30–31)

This *hadith*, named "the *hadith* of Gabriel", has been keenly interpreted by mystics and theologians alike. Faith is attestation by heart, by tongue and by limbs, that is by knowledge (*islam*), by reasoning (*iman*) and by action (*ihsan*). The domain of knowledge is spirit (*ruh*); the domain of reasoning is intellect ('*aql*); the domain of action is jurisprudence (*shari'a*) (see Chittick 2000).

Despite the eminence of spiritual dimension, Islam is essentially orthopraxis—that is, practice (right behavior or *ihsan*) of the five pillars of faith. The most important of the five pillars is the belief that there is no other god than God and Muhammad is his Messenger (in the formula of the Arabic *shahada*). The two parts of the *shahada* do not appear together in the Qur'an, but verse 37.35 states that "there is no other god than God" (*la ilah illa Allah*), while verse 48.29 states that "Muhammad is the Messenger of God" (*Muhammad rasul Allah*). Thus the profession of faith can be brought together from various parts of the Qur'an. But Islam is more than the profession of faith; it is also—as we have said—*complete surrender and belief in the will of God*, and this is the primary meaning as well as the ordinary meaning of the term "Islam". There is also a second fundamental implication. The God to whom one surrenders is One, and the Unity of God unifies the reality of nature and the same reality of humanity. This philosophical principle is very well described by the Muslim Brother Sayyid Qutb (1906–1966), the author of a fundamental commentary on the Qur'an to which we shall return in the fifth chapter of this volume:

Islam is the religion of unification, and it is difficult to overemphasize this point. The religion of unity is very much centred around the notion of *tawhid* or unity as a central aspect of Islam. It means the Unity of God, the unification of all the religions in the religion of God, the uniformity of the message transmitted from all the prophets since the start of life.

(Shepard 1996: 33)

And also:

> The essence of life, with all its various species, is one, and the essence of
> man, with all the infinite human varieties and potentialities, is one. [. . .]
> The unique sweep of Islam is to determine the meaning of God's wor-
> ship in human life according to the Qur'an. [. . .] The realization of this
> human sweep remains impossible so long as we distinguish between the
> material and the spiritual parts of our lives. We should appreciate that
> our consciousness and our actions are part of a harmonious and single
> entity. Our notion of the Unity of God ought to reflect our ability to bring
> together and unify the various aspects of our life.
>
> (Qutb 1991: 104–107 passim)

In the light of these considerations, we need to return to the issue
of whether and how religion (*din*) is really connected to the "world"
(*dunya*) since there are no distinctions between the acts of worship
and social acts of behavior. It follows, Qutb writes, that

> Islam is the religion that unifies the act of worship and the social act,
> dogma and law, spirit and matter, economic and essential values, this
> and the next life, earth and heaven.
>
> (Shepard 1996: 33)

So Islam is both religion and (secular) world (*din wa dunya*). The
great theologian al-Ghazali (1058–1111) has accordingly pointed out
how exterior and interior aspects of human reality correspond and
reflect each other, so that the legal practice of acts of worship work
to purify and perfect the soul. It would not be superfluous to quote
this long section of the *Book of Forty Principles of Religion*:

> Know that the key to happiness is following the Sunna (behaviour) and
> imitating the Apostle of God in all his comings and goings, motion, and
> rest even as regards his eating, rising, sleeping and speaking. I do not say
> this only in regard to his practice in the arts of worship (*adab al-'ibadat*),
> for there is no reason for neglecting the practices (*al-Sunan*) which
> appear therein, rather I say this in all matters of customs. Thus there
> results the absolute following [of Muhammad]. Allah said, "If you love
> God, follow me; God will love you". And Allah also said, "Whatever the
> Prophet gave you, take it, and whatever he forbids you, desist from it".

It is incumbent upon you to put on full trousers (*al-sarawil*) while sitting and to attire yourself with a turban while standing. It is also incumbent upon you that, when you put on your shoes, you begin with the right foot; that you eat with your right hand; that you cut your fingernails beginning with the forefinger of the right hand and ending with the thumb of the right hand; that you begin with the little toe with the right foot and finish with the little toe of the left foot. Thus in all your movement and rest. Moreover you must not show levity in regard to these matters and say that these things relate only to customs and that there is no meaning in following them. For if you do this, there will close against you a great door of the doors of happiness.

Now, perhaps you desire at this moment to know the reasons for striving for the following in regard to these activities and you may consider it farfetched to suppose that there is an important matter underlying this topic. Know, therefore, that the mentioning of the secrets in regard to every one of these practices is long, and though it is not the purpose of this book to explain them, it is necessary that you understand that the Sunna contains secrets.

(al-Ghazali 1970: 102–103)

We should not be surprised that faith includes rules about dressing, eating or how to cut toe nails, since rectitude in exterior behavior is the precondition for rectitude of the spirit and soul. Many medieval theologians like Ibn Taymiyya (1263–1328) and especially the modern radical Muslims like the already mentioned Sayyid Qutb have argued that Islam is both a religion and a political system since in Islam one can see a strict integration between religion and politics. In a book like this on the Qur'an, political issues do not concern us directly. However, it is important to underline that—if Islam is for all the believers a religion and a world, and for a few followers a religion and a state (*dawla*)—it is as much *din* as it is ideology. Here ideology is meant in the positive sense of the term—that is, as abstract and universal thought about reality. It is true, though, that one (like Marx and many Marxists) can treat ideology as like alienation or false consciousness, as manipulation by lies. But it is obvious, according to Ferruccio Rossi Landi, that ideology may be both action and social planning: "[L]ike a real social force, all ideology is capable of pervading society in which it is formed" (Rossi Landi 1978: 5). If it is true that Islam is a religion and universe, then it is ideology in the sense of a specific outlook pervading human life and influencing the nature of social organization (and this is broadly Gramsci's opinion).

In order to present itself completely as a positive ideology, Islam has to take on board its historical background. A highly significant aspect of classical Islamic culture consists of what has been taken up in modern times as a result of an anti-utopian conception of history, or of a retrospective utopia. By this expression I mean the tendency to consider the past, especially the period of Muhammad and the first caliphs, as a perfect and incomparable golden age in which the connection between religion and politics, ethics and the community had been successfully realized to produce a perfect Islamic society. Such a golden age can be used as an exemplar, as something to be repeated perhaps, and as an argument against innovation and modernization. This anti-utopian (or retrospective utopian) strategy is clearly expressed in classical times by Hanbalite thinkers from Ibn Hanbal himself to Ibn Batta and Ibn Taymiyya, and in contemporary times by radical Muslims such as Sayyid Qutb and al-Mawdudi. The anti-utopian strategy can lead to and encourage the project of separating the sacred text from history. Removing the sacred text from history means, on the one hand, not linking it with the changing socio-political changes in which people live and, on the other, solidifying its meaning in just one direction (treating the text as having only one kind of meaning). We shall see in the fifth chapter of this volume how some contemporary Qur'anic exegetes have tried to take a different approach by seeking to locate the Qur'an in history.

THE CHARACTERISTICS OF ISLAM AS A RELIGION

For Muslims, Islam is the natural religion of humanity (*fitra* or *hanifiyya*), a religion in which every individual is born. There is a hadith of the Prophet that says: "Every person is born in the natural religion. It is his/her parents who make him/her a Christian, a Jew or a Zoroastrian". This conception finds support in the Qur'anic verse 30.30 that Bausani translates in a way that could be rendered in English as "Turn steadfastly to the true religion, in purity of faith (*hanifan*), the original nature (*fitra*) in which God made men" (Bausani 1988: 297). Bonelli by contrast translates it as "Whoever turns his face steadfastly to the true religion, the *hanif* [monotheist]; it is the institution of God to which He has made men naturally inclined" (Bonelli 1976: 376). For his part, Arberry translates *fitra* as "God's original" (Arberry 1982: 414). Abdel Haleem has this: "[A]s a man of pure faith, stand firm. . . . This is the natural disposition God instilled in mankind" (Abdel Haleem 2004: 258). Each spontaneous tendency to monotheism is shaped as a natural religion, through which, although it might seem to be paradoxical, the authentic Jew and the authentic Christian are really "Muslims".

For Muslims, Islam is a prophetic religion, one that, like Judaism and Christianity, is based on the idea that the message of God is said to have been revealed through the sending of prophets. The prophetic story starts with Adam, the "father of human beings", and continues by Noah, Abraham (the "Friend of God") who was not a Jew but a pure monotheist (3.67), and then by Moses (the prophet of the Jews) and Jesus. These prophets are called the five legislators of humanity, five people who have brought a Book containing the revelations and commandments of God. The Book of Moses is called the Torah, while that of Jesus is called the Gospel. The content of the Torah and the Gospel were originally entirely similar. The prophetic revelation is really an expression of the human mind, the natural inclination of humanity being monotheism. The Torah and the Gospel are however said to have been "falsified" by the Jews and the Christians (*tahrif* is the term used by Muslim theologians to highlight this falsification and means primarily "to alter the words"). This is the reason, for example, why Muslims talk of the Gospel and not the Gospels. According to divine revelation, there was only one Gospel; the fact that there are four (or more) Gospels proves that the Christians have arbitrarily manipulated the original single revelation. The Jews and the Christians have really betrayed the message of their prophets, through whom God had warned of the need to send a sixth legislative prophet with a new Book. This was obviously to be Muhammad and the Qur'an.

Islam represents itself as being the essence of the earlier revelations, the most perfect and so in effect abrogated Judaism and Christianity. This view is shared equally by the Sunnis and the Shiites, who are divided on the issue of the succession to the Prophet. The Shiites think that the imams are the successors of 'Ali, cousin and son-in-law of Muhammad and fourth caliph after him. The imams are in a position to furnish an esoteric interpretation of Scripture, while the Sunnis are more likely to accept the literal meaning of the text. This is the first time that the problem of interpretation, the critical central issue of this book, is raised in relation to the historical aspects of the doctrinal disputes between the Sunni and the Shiites.

Islam is predominantly an anti-dogmatic religion, with just two general assumptions. There is a very basic profession of faith, and an absence of an ecclesiastical judge and a central doctrinal authority. In fact, the only principle to which all Muslims must agree is this assertion of the profession of faith: "There is no god but God and Muhammad is the Messenger of God". This is the indispensable belief; everything else, at least from a theoretical perspective, is supererogatory or more than what is required. The study of theology is inessential. Instead, what binds Muslims is the practice of acts of worship, the "five pillars" consisting of the profession of faith, prayer, fasting, pilgrimage and charity. In fact, as we have said, Islam is really an orthopraxy. In order to be saved, it is necessary to act.

The fact that there are not sacraments in Islam and that dogma is resolved in orthopraxy renders a priestly class redundant. The connection between God and the believer is direct and immediate. The function of priests is replaced in Islam by *ulama*, experts in law and the religious sciences who are appointed jurists and theologians rather than priests. This means that an expert jurist may express legal opinions that are binding not on everyone but only on those who adhere to the school of law of that jurist. However, Muslims say with pride that they do not have a Church, and instead have constantly accepted the widest possible scope for debate and subjective and personal opinion.

THE QUR'AN AND INTERPRETATION

The concept of *din* has been summarized here. The Qur'an constitutes the expressive space of *din*, the linguistic system in which *din* is worked out. It enables us to talk about theology, prophecy, eschatology and ethical moral and political principles. The prominence of the legal and practical aspect is what many Muslims say makes Islam a religion empty of "mystery", empty of those aspects that cannot be justified by human reason (like the incarnation or Eucharist in Christianity or in Catholicism) and that form between the believer and God a gap that only interpretation and knowledge mediation can bridge. In this sense, the Qur'anic method is essentially a practical and juridical method. This idea is expressed vigorously by a powerful Indian thinker Muhammad Iqbal (1873–1938), later on regarded as the major thinker of Pakistan, who wrote:

> The most remarkable fact about the Qur'an is the importance that is reserved to reality in the sense of what may be observed. [. . .] This empirical attitude of the Qur'an produces in its followers a sentiment of respect for the facts and makes them definite builders of modern science. [. . .] The Qur'an celebrates change. The culture of Asia and the whole of antiquity failed because it pursued reality exclusively from the inside and moved from the internal towards the external. [. . .] Qur'anic naturalism consists in recognizing that man is bound up with nature.
>
> (Iqbal 1968: 20ff.)

The spirit of the Qur'an—Iqbal said—is anti-classic. Alessandro Bausani, one of the greatest Italian Islamologists of the twentieth century, pointed out that Iqbal had thus emphasized the rational character of Islam and the experimental and positive nature of the Qur'anic method: "The meaning of Qur'anic revelation is not a revelation of mysteries. God leads Muhammad to say in the Qur'an: 'I do not know the hidden', the mystery, the transcendent which He evidently did not reveal to him. On the contrary, revelation is a practical method in order to change the world. To a degree it is more of a praxis than a philosophy or a cosmology. Many problems and pseudo-problems of Islamic cultural history can be resolved or better dissolved if we bear in mind this radical aspect of the legal and practical nature of Qur'anic revelation" (Bausani 1973: 724).

In fact, this is a unique characteristic of Islamic revelation. The Qur'an certainly refers to the "key to secrets", but the "secret" (the term *ghayb* really means "that which cannot be seen") is really contained "in a clear Book" (*kitab mubin*), the Qur'an itself. The central verse is perhaps 6.59: "God has the keys of the secret [what is invisible] and only He knows them. God knows what there is on the earth and in the sea. Not a leaf falls without his knowledge, there is not a grain in the dark of the land or anything green or dried out that is not [written] in a clear Book".

To interpret the Book means at the same time to interpret the secret since the ultimate knowledge of everything only belongs to God.

This is how and why the sacred Book assumes its specific role, and so its authentic meaning is framed in a series of systematically reciprocal connections with other factors. After all the Qur'an is a linguistic system in which the meaning of each concept is represented by the function it has within Qur'anic language as a whole. So for example it is not possible to define the concept of Spirit (*ruh*) separately from that of order (*amr*), and the Qur'an says: "The Spirit comes from the Order of my Lord" (17.85). Spirit and Order converge in representing the Qur'anic knitted-structured and rational cosmology, and each internal issue like this has a precise terminology that represents an interconnected structure, a construction established internally. One of the best-known modern exegetes of the Qur'an, the Egyptian 'A'isha Bint al-Shati' has suggested that each word of the Qur'an is selected with great care and is just right for the context in which it is found, so that it is not possible to substitute a synonym without the risk of invalidating or damaging the text. This is a theme of the claims often made about the Qur'an in medieval Muslim studies, that some parts of the Qur'an cannot be swapped for others (as argued by Subhi al-Salih, a contemporary commentator to whom we shall turn later). For example Averroes in the *Decisive Treatise* said, "Whenever a statement in Scripture conflicts in its apparent meaning with a conclusion of demonstration, if Scripture is considered carefully, and the rest of its contents searched page by page, there will invariably be found among the expressions of Scripture something which in its apparent meaning bears witness to that allegorical interpretation" (Averroes 1976: 51). It is a matter of the self-referentiality of Qur'anic language that seems to establish the text has a determinate meaning. But this is not really the case. The specific role of the words used within the Qur'anic context do not rule out the idea that Scripture is open to a plurality of meanings. In fact the opposite is true. The plurality of meanings in which the *ghayb*—the "mystery" or, better, the "un-seen"—can be understood lies precisely in the Qur'anic language and the Qur'anic context. This idea seems right and demonstrates that, when the Qur'anic text is studied, it is not necessary to cut off interpretation. We need to look carefully at what is involved in drawing limits to interpretation, something that in philosophy is called the hermeneutic method, and it involves not only the letters and the comments of the text but also the link between the text itself and a precise conception of the world and reality.

The aim of this book is, on the one hand, to offer a clear exposition of the form and content of the Qur'an and, on the other, to convey an understanding of the methods and directions that interpretation followed in the Islamic world and after the orientalists. If we try to see first how Muslims have interpreted the meaning of their sacred text and how the classical science of interpretation may regard that text as open, then we can see in the contemporary world what theoretical possibilities may apply to our understanding of the text.

SUMMARY

In this chapter we have dealt with

- The meaning of religion in Islam.
- The link between inner and outward aspects of human life and how they are related to each other.
- In what sense Islam is an ideology.
- The features of Islam as a natural, monotheistic, prophetic, scriptural and anti-dogmatic religion.
- The importance of Qur'anic interpretation in approaching the text successfully.

REFERENCES/READINGS

Abdel Haleem, M. *The Qur'an*, Oxford University Press, Oxford 2004.

Arberry, A. *The Koran Interpreted*, Oxford University Press, Oxford 1982.

Averroes, *On the Harmony of Religion and Philosophy*, trans. G. Hourani, Luzac, London 1976.

Bausani, A. "Scienza e religione nell'Islam", *Scientia* LXVII, 1973, pp. 723–746.

Bausani, A. *Il Corano*, BUR Rizzoli, Milano 1988.

Bonelli, L. *Il Corano*, Hoepli, Milano 1976.

Boullata, I. "Modern Qur'an Exegesis. A Study of Bint al-Shati Method", *The Muslim World* LXIV, 1979, pp. 103–113.

Campanini, M. *Islam e Politica*, Il Mulino, Bologna 2015.

Chittick, W. *Sufism*, Oneworld, Oxford 2000.

Filoramo, G. *Che cos'è la Religione*, Einaudi, Torino 2004.

Gardet, L. *Entry din in Encyclopedie de l'Islam*, 2nd edition, vol. II, Brill, Leiden 1961.

Al-Ghazali, *Kitab al-Arba'in fi usul al-din (Book of the Forty Principles of Religion)*, Maktabat al-Jindi, Cairo 1970.

Al-Ghazali, Deliverance from Error, in W.M. Watt (ed.), *The Faith and Practice of Al-Ghazali*, Oneworld, Oxford 1994.

Halm, H. *Shiism*, Edinburgh University Press, Edinburgh 1991.

Hodgson, M. *The Venture of Islam*, Chicago University Press, Chicago 1973.

Iqbal, M. *Reconstruction of Religious Thought in Islam*, Muhammad Ashraf, Lahore 1968.

Al-Nawawi, *Il giardino dei devoti*, a cura di A. Scarabel, Società Italiana Testi Islamici, Trieste 1990.

Qutb, S. *The Islamic Concept and Its Characteristics*, American Trust Publications, Indianapolis 1991.

Rossi Landi, F. *Ideologia*, Isedi, Milano 1978.

Shepard, W. *Sayyid Qutb and Islamic Activism: A Translation and Critical Analysis of "Social Justice in Islam"*, Brill, Leiden 1996.

2

STRUCTURE AND COMPOSITION

THE AUTHORSHIP OF THE QUR'AN

What issues arise when we consider the composition and reception of the Qur'an as a message? We should say immediately that to talk of the "composition" of the Qur'an is liable to lead to misunderstanding. The author of the Qur'an for Muslims is God, who certainly did not sit down at a table to write it. For Muslims it is absolutely unacceptable and a serious blasphemy to say that the author of the Qur'an is the Prophet Muhammad. The Qur'an exists, we are told, eternally with God. In the Logos of God, his speech or Word, the Qur'an, can be considered as emanating from God. In the first centuries of Islamic theology (ninth to tenth CE), it was possible to debate the creation of even the Qur'an, in particular the issue of whether the word of God is eternal or otherwise. For the majority of Muslims, and certainly what could be called the orthodox position, the Qur'an is considered eternal, but this conclusion is not without difficulty. The defenders of the idea that the Qur'an was created were the Mu'tazilites (a school of thinkers influenced by Greek philosophy that flourished in Iraq in the ninth century CE). They argued that the Qur'an was created since, if it were eternal, it would exist with God as though it were another eternal thing, and this would constitute a second God (something similar to a Trinitarian hypostasis), and this multiplication of eternal things runs the risk of ending in polytheism. The thesis of the uncreated nature of the sacred Book was defended mainly by the Ash'arites (important in the tenth century CE), one of the authoritative groups in classical Islamic thought, according to which God expresses Himself through words that are separate from his essence, but in a way that "we do not know". The Ash'arite position has triumphed finally and has come to be considered "orthodox", in the sense that it is accepted by the majority of the community, but the issue of the eternity or otherwise of the Qur'an is not only a theological dispute. The Mu'tazilite doctrine was in fact supported by the 'Abbasid caliph al-Ma'mun (r. 813–833 CE), who made it state doctrine and used the doctrine of the created Qur'an as a test to determine the loyalty of those who had to choose between supporting either his leadership or religious orthodoxy. The caliph wanted to link his authority with the belief in the created Qur'an and exercise a sort of caesaro-papism: he would have concentrated in his hands both the civil and the religious authority. In fact, the notion that the Qur'an is created and so came to be modified, perhaps in line with the political exigencies of the time, gives the caliphate a freedom of intervention that the intangibility and eternity of the text would not allow. The victory of the Ash'arite thesis helped to cement the class of 'ulama as the theological and legal guardians of the Law, although their influence on the state turned out to be relatively minor. Actually, caliphs and sultans searched for the endorsement by the 'ulama but remained fully independent from religious control.

The problem of the creation of the Qur'an is apparently a strictly theological problem, but nowadays it resumed its political importance. A few among the most innovative contemporary Muslim thinkers, like Muhammad 'Abduh (1849–1905) and Nasr Abu Zayd (1943–2010) (discussed later also in Chapter 5 in this volume), professed to be neo-Mu'tazilites sharing the doctrine of the Qur'an's creation—for an updated and easier exegesis of the text would have deep outcomes in legislation, organization of society, scientific outlook and so on, releasing all the potentialities of hermeneutics.

The Book refers in verses 13.39 and 85.22 to what appears to be a heavenly archetype of the Book existing eternally with God, which seems to support the Ash'arite solution (we will return to this argument in Chapter 4 in this volume). In any case, whether the Qur'an is eternal or otherwise, for Muslims God is the author and Muhammad the Prophet is the recipient. Muhammad did not "compose" the Qur'an. He is limited to receiving it and communicating it to his companions and disciples. So we possess a volume, a book that in some way is said to be arranged and transmitted in an unalterable way. In this sense we have to deal with a "composition" of the Qur'an. As we deal with such a topic, it is worth discussing an issue that is often regarded as "revisionist" and orientalist (see below and Chapter 4 in this volume), the reconstruction of how Muslims think in line with this issue that has just been discussed.

THE "COMPOSITION" OF THE QUR'AN

Originally revelation was broadcast by word of mouth and was memorized by the faithful. Muhammad communicated with his closest companions, and the message was diffused more widely then to the community. After all, Bedouin culture was essentially oral, and the poetry competitions that were popular in Mecca during the fairs and pilgrimages did not depend on having anything written down. The question is important since it is linked with another problem that is very relevant. Did Muhammad know how to read and write? Did he know how to write down the revelations that he received? The opinion of Muslims is that Muhammad was illiterate. This is how the term *ummi* is interpreted, referred to Muhammad in the Qur'an twice at 7.157 and 158. Western scholars, naturally, find this puzzling. Bausani, for example, translates the term *ummi* as "gentile" (i.e., "non-Jew") and suggests the most plausible interpretation seems to be that the term *ummi* involves being identified ethnically not as a Jew but rather as an Arab. A. T. Welch has argued that *nabi ummi* means a prophet belonging to a people who were not primary recipients of a Scripture, representing a discontinuity with the Jewish/Christian context that had been the recipient of the earlier revelations. Arberry's translation of the term *ummi* is "Prophet of the common folk".

The "illiteracy" of the Prophet is important from an Islamic perspective since it confirms the extraordinary miracle of the transmission dealing with the reception of a text that is pure and perfect like the Qur'an by a man who did not even possess the rudiments of reading and writing. Western orientalism generally upholds that Muhammad possessed some idea of the letters, since he had after all worked as a merchant for many years. Whether he was illiterate or not, there is evidence that fragments of text, single verses, part of chapters (suras) and so on were during the life of the Prophet outlined using whatever was available, such as bits of earthenware, stones, animal bones and leaves. So it is clear that this would fit in with the idea that the main way of memorizing and transmitting the Qur'an would still be oral.

Now, in the successive wars that followed the death of Muhammad, many guardians of the Qur'an (*huffaz*), many of those who knew it by memory without having to make recourse to the written script, died. This led the famous Companion 'Umar, who had become the second caliph, to persuade the first caliph, Abu Bakr (r. 632–634), to take steps that would ensure that the revelation did not become lost. Abu Bakr was initially unwilling to do what Muhammad had not wanted to do, but he instructed a freed slave of Muhammad, Zayd ibn Thabit, to collect and organize the "sheets" (*suhuf*) on which the various fragments of the Qur'an had been variously preserved, and he supervised the collection in line with the oral evidence of the Companions.

The initiative of Abu Bakr did not immediately result in a definitive edition and what we might call a "composition" of the Qur'an. In various towns of the Arab empire, which was just becoming established, there were other versions of it that were held by famous companions and friends of the Prophet. Some of these—like those by 'Abdallah ibn 'Abbas, by Ubayy (in Syria) and especially by Ibn Mas'ud (in Kufa)—had particular authority. These versions differed in quite substantial aspects. Apart from differences in letters, they changed the number of the suras, their order and their titles, and really their content also. The gravity of the situation convinced the third caliph, 'Uthman (r. 644–656), to institute a commission with the participation of Zayd ibn Thabit, which worked swiftly on preparing what might be called an *editio princeps*, a master edition. The result was perhaps rather longer than satisfactory, because the Arabic language of the time was not yet perfected. Lacking vocalization and diacritical marks, it left open the possibility of confusing and making mistakes about many words. However, the 'Uthman organization of the text or redaction determined definitely the order and the length of the chapters that we still read today. It is the so-called *Vulgata*, the basic canon transmitted over the centuries. The caliph took four (or in another version six) copies of the agreed text of the commission and installed them in four large cities of the empire: Mecca, Kufa, Basra and Damascus. He ordered the destruction of the earlier versions.

The majority tradition said that the initiative of ʿUthman was well received, and even ʿAli, an enemy of ʿUthman for political reasons, accepted it. However, those who thought they understood the text better resisted. Ibn Masʿud in particular refused to obey the caliph's injunction and continued to defend the greater legitimacy of his own evidence. However, over time the various versions of the Qurʾan stabilized around the ʿUthman version, which came to be preserved and treated with great respect. The supporters of ʿAli who came to be designated the Shiites argued that ʿUthman and his followers had suppressed the authentic Qurʾanic text that had prioritized the role of their chief—that is, ʿAli. ʿAli and ʿUthman argued over the caliphate, and a huge debate arose over the claims of the different political groups. In order to resolve this issue, a lot of attention was paid to the different readings that could be made of the Arabic text. It is enough to give two examples. The verse 75.17 reads, in the Vulgate of ʿUthman: "It is for us (*ʿalayna*) to collect [it]". However, a Shiite rendering of this passage attributes to Ibn Masʿud slightly different phrasing: "It is for our ʿAli (*ʿaliyyuna*) to collect [it]". Similarly, the verse 35.56 officially goes, "God and his angels pray for (*ʿala*) the Prophet", while the Shiite version goes, "God and the angels link ʿAli and the Prophet". It is only a slight change of letter that produces a very different meaning, and as a result it transforms profoundly the religious role given to ʿAli, an equal or even superior role to that of Muhammad.

Shiite tradition affirms that the same ʿAli collected his own version of the Qurʾan, obviously—at least in Shiite eyes—more reliable than the ʿUthman's one. This collection has disappeared however, and it is very important to emphasize that despite what we have said, the Shiites accepted ʿUthman's *Vulgata* as valid and pray with the ʿUthman's Qurʾan.

No really important developments occurred under the regime of the first Umayyads, but by the end of the seventh century the governor of Iraq al-Hajjaj promoted a fixed text, a final rendition of the Qurʾanic text, with the vocalization and diacritic marks that could end not only the disputes about meaning but also systematized

Arabic orthography. Naturally, al-Hajjaj was accused by the Shiites of being the person responsible for deforming the text by allowing the Sunnis to deny the legitimate role of 'Ali. The process of putting together the definitive Qur'anic text took longer and became complex and disputatious, and, according to Regis Blachère (1977), at the start of the eleventh century we cannot talk of a completely final version, but during that century we can find the definitive form of the Qur'an that we possess today. Bell and Watt, on the other hand, think that the process of development of Scripture was completed by the end of the ninth century.

New recent discoveries have anticipated the dating of the final version of the Qur'an. First of all, a surely authentic palimpsest found in the great mosque of Sanaa in Yemen has been dated roughly about 670 (see Sadeghi and Bergmann 2010; and Sadeghi and Goudarzi 2012). Second, the Qur'anic inscription in the Dome of the Rock in Jerusalem, built under the Umayyad caliph 'Abd al-Malik (r. 685–705), confirms that a Qur'anic text circulated under some kind of form in that period. Third, in July 2015, a Qur'anic manuscript analyzed by an *équipe* of Birmingham University has been dated by the first decades of the seventh century: being contemporary of the Prophet's life, it could represent a (at least partial) confirmation of traditional Muslim account.

From a religious point of view, the earlier debate on the many possible versions of the text has left an important result. The tradition affirms the existence of seven readings all equally legal and canonical. In spite of this the text is fixed definitively, although there are some possible phonetic variations, some differences in techniques of recitation that lead to slight modifications in the textual style of writing. None of these modifications, it is generally agreed, have any significance for the dogmatic and doctrinal teaching of the Book. For example, it is not very important in verse 40.21 if we read that "they were stronger than you (*minkum*)" as compared with "they were stronger than them (*minhum*)". In the verse 2.219 we can read that "in them is a grave (*kabir*) sin" or instead "in them is much (*kathir*) sin". These variants in the letters have significant implications only for the recitation of the text on liturgical occasions. The seven readings are generally accepted (but some talk about ten or even forty), and three of them are attributed to the reciters (*qari'*) of Kufa, and one each to the reciters of Mecca, Medina, Basra and Damascus.

The timeline that we have reconstructed for the composition of the Qur'an reflects for the most part, and not as precisely as we may have suggested, Muslims' own opinions about the formation of their sacred text. On many issues this reconstruction is accepted also by European and American orientalists, but there are disagreements on specific issues. For example, the fact that we have already discussed that 'Umar convinced Abu Bakr to establish an unalterable version of the revelation, we know to be contradicted by various venerable and strong pieces of evidence. Abu Bakr may have started the work and 'Umar completed it, or it could be that the latter got the whole enterprise going. Traditional history is completely clear in saying that there is a unique and unalloyed "authentic" version of the Qur'an conveyed to Muhammad and passed on finally to 'Uthman.

Moreover, some scholars have pointed out that the Arabic of the Qur'an is not the Arabic spoken by the Quraysh (the tribe to which Muhammad belonged), and so it is possible to doubt whether the book really did not change at all in the hands of the commission instituted by 'Uthman. An even more devastating critique has been put forward by orientalists like Christoph Luxenberg (a pseudonym) and Gabriel Said Reynolds. Luxenberg (2000) tried to demonstrate that the obscure expressions and odd words of the Qur'an become perfectly clear if the reader has recourse to Aramaic rather than Arabic because the Qur'an was originally a collection of paraphrased translation of Syriac texts. Luxenberg bends and forces the Qur'anic text in services of his aims, sometimes considering obscure verses that are perfectly clear; but the point is that, if he is right, the Qur'an would result in a patent falsification. Gabriel Reynolds (2010) argues that the Qur'an is a homiletic text built on the basis of a previous Biblical subtext: this thesis, besides minimizing the originality of the Islamic message and reducing the core of Qur'anic revelation to a Biblical matrix, implicitly contests the reliability of the Qur'an as religious and historical source, for example of Muhammad's life.

We can talk about different textual traditions from which the 'Uthman Vulgate was composed through a process of formation of the text that was originally complex, long and broken up. The orientalists continue to ask questions about this, with little interest aroused among Muslims. It is important to bring up again, with Alford T. Welch, that after the tenth century, during which many works on the history of the Qur'anic text were written by Muslims, people lost interest in this subject, and the 'Uthmanian Vulgate acquired its institutional status that it still possesses today and is regarded as having absolute authenticity.

THE STRUCTURE OF THE QUR'AN

The Qur'an that we possess today in 'Uthman's version is laid out in terms of chapters (in Arabic, a chapter is a sura), of which there are 114, and in turn the chapters are divided into verses (in Arabic, *ayat*). Each sura contains a variable number of verses that go from 286 in the 2nd sura (The Cow) to 3 in the 108th sura (The Abundance). The verses themselves also differ in length. Some contain little more than a word, while others occupy the space of a page. The Qur'an is curiously arranged; the suras are not in chronological order, the order in which they were revealed, but in an order of length. Most of the longer chapters are at the beginning, and most of the shorter ones at the end. The criterion of organization is not rigid but in general takes this form. The reasons for this anomaly that have been produced are not entirely convincing, not even to Muslim exegetes.

Muslim and Western exegetes each distinguish between two periods of revelation, the Meccan (when the Prophet Muhammad lived in Mecca from 610 at the start of the revelation to 622) and the Medinan period (after the Hijra and up to the death of the Prophet, from 622 to 632). The Meccan revelations can be broken up into three periods, but not all Muslims accept the details of this organization of the periods, and some think that it is only useful to think of these revelations in terms of one period. A contemporary thinker—for example, the Lebanese Sobhi al-Salih—has managed to distinguish between three Meccan periods and also three Medinan. The Medinan revelations can really seem more compact than the Meccan, since at Medina the Prophet Muhammad was not only a Prophet but also a head of state and organizer of the Community. The revelations often take on the character of a systematic codification.

There are three phases of the Meccan period. First of all, from 610 to 615, Muhammad started off on his mission and organized his first followers. The revelation in favor of the Unity of God against polytheism took an increasingly eschatological form and denounced the wickedness and immorality of humanity. It became a message with both an ethical and a spiritual content. Persecutions against the new faith in the commercial and materialistic environment of Mecca were sporadic, but hostility seems to have increased as time went on. The second phase went from 615 to 619 and was the period of the greatest difficulty for Muhammad. The persecution became ever more severe. The Prophet worked hard to recruit followers and allies. He had lost in a crisis solidarity with his tribe and clan. His defenders and supporters of the first phase, his uncle Abu Talib and wife Khadija, died. The revelation started to center more on stories of former patriarchs and the continuity of the prophetic chain. Muhammad presents an account of his appropriate role. The third phase went from 619 to 622. These were the years of a change in fortune. Some of the inhabitants of Medina were converted to Islam. They invited Muhammad to intervene as a judge in the factional struggles that divide the city. Since the persecutions in Mecca were becoming tougher and even threatened the life of the Prophet, Muhammad decided to move to Medina and to build up there the Community of true believers. The Hegira, the "emigration", took place in 622, the first year of the Islamic calendar. In the third period, revelation reflected the break with the past and the necessity of assuming a strategy that would fix the nature of the Community once and for all. In relation to historical facts and the orientation assumed by revelation, the Qur'an revealed in Mecca demonstrates diversity in a number of ways, in particular in style, language and of course in theme.

In Medina, as we have seen, he set up the bases of civil society in accordance with the rules of the new religion of Islam. The message now starts to concentrate a bit more on social and practical themes. And in Medina, while struggles and wars were bursting out between believers and Meccan pagans, the decision to fight became irreversible, not putting up passively with persecution but reacting against it. Warfare did not stop theological reflection, however. Some of the passages from this Medinan period express intense spiritual fervor, as in the Throne verses and the Light verses (discussed below).

It is important to grasp that the Meccan suras are more numerous than the Medinan and take up more than two thirds of the text in length. Many of the longer ones are Medinan, like the second (The Cow), which is absolutely the longest, and the third, fourth and fifth. These four suras take up about eighty pages out of a total of about four hundred. The suras, in the original Arabic, have a title that shows whether they are Meccan or Medinan. There are verses recognized as Medinan in Meccan suras and verses recognized as Meccan in Medinan suras, but it is practically impossible to reconstruct exactly when they were revealed. This issue is carefully dealt with in the Arabic editions of the Book. This led to a state-organized exegetical project that resulted in the standard contemporary edition in Egypt in the reign of King Fu'ad in 1923. It considered the first sura to be 96 (Clot of Blood) and the last 110 (Triumph). We are following here the numeration of the verses of the Vulgate of Fu'ad, but some Muslim scholars consider as revealed first the verses 1–7 of sura 74 (The Wrapped Up One), and other scholars, when translating the Qur'an, have arranged them in different ways. For example, many of the older translators such as the Italian Bonelli or the English Arberry both follow the numeration of Flügel, a German scholar who edited the text in 1834.

Another division by Muslims of their sacred Book is the ordering for liturgical reasons of it into thirty parts (*juz'*) roughly equal in length. This division is extremely useful especially during the sacred month of fasting, Ramadan, because the Qur'an can be read in a way that is aligned with the appropriate time, and each of the thirty parts can be read on each of the thirty days of the month. (The Islamic calendar is lunar and composed of some months of twenty-nine days and some of thirty days. As the lunar year is shorter than the solar, the months do not correspond to seasons as with the Western calendar. So the fasting time can occur in any season of the year, from spring to winter. Fasting during the very hot summer months in Arabia or in other non-temperate countries could be very hard.)

LITERARY AND LINGUISTIC ASPECTS

The exterior form of the Qur'an that we possess places great importance on language. The study of Qur'anic Arabic is a study replete with sacred value. Some aspects of the text cohere with this. One of the most intriguing is that of the "separate letters" or "open letters" that appear at the beginning of some suras. For example, sura 2 (The Cow) starts with three suspended letters: Alif, Lam, Mim. The same three letters appear in the text in five suras (3, 29, 30, 31, 32). Another frequent combination is Alif, Lam, Ra, which appears in five suras (10, 11, 12, 14, 15), and another still is Ha, Mim, which comes in the text consecutively in suras 40 to 46. In total there are fourteen different combinations. The exegetes, whether Muslim or Western, have strained greatly to produce explanations of these mysterious signs. Some have argued that they are allusions to the divine attributes; others, that they are acronyms of the transmitters of the Qur'an. It is also possible that they are "titles" that were used to name particular suras that were similar to each other, but that over time became separated from their original references. The fact that only sura 9 fails to start with the formula "In the name of God, the most gracious, the merciful", which comes at the start of the other 113, has given rise to the idea that originally the ninth sura may have been part of the eighth. In any case, what is interesting about the "separate letters" is that they have acquired a symbolic value, so much so that some exegetes, suspecting the presence of divine mystery, have refused to speculate on the issue, to such a degree that the mystics have turned the issue into a source of esoteric interpretation.

The Qur'an is a Book that has to be recited. It is a Book that contains parables and edifying stories, moral suasion and stories of prophets and kings. But a significant issue of how to approach the text lies in its literary form. It is not possible any longer to avoid this issue, which has led to the flowing of rivers of ink and which has been addressed by so many Muslim and Western authors. A good example of a "traditional" Muslim approach is given in Sayyid Qutb's *Al-taswir al-fanni fi'l-Qur'an* (*The Artistic Shape of the Qur'an*), while Muhammad Arkoun and Nasr Hamid Abu Zayd pursue the topic of the literary character of the Qur'an using a similar approach to Western orientalism. It is necessary to raise a pair of questions: how the language of the Qur'an specifically contributes to its rhythm and musicality, and the inimitability of the Book.

Muslims, especially if they are Arab, claim that reciting the holy Book is to be suffused with the splendor and rhythmicity of the language. In effect, if we study the suras of the Qur'an or at least the brief suras where the verses are concise and follow a real rhyming assonance, it is possible to verify the literary character of the Book. We can limit ourselves to some examples. The "Opening" (the first sura in the Qur'an) is particularly important for worship since it constitutes the basis of prayer, rather as though it were the Lord's Prayer of Islam. Al-Ghazali states that the "Opening" opens the eight doors of Paradise, and a mystical thinker like Hasan al-Basri (seventh to eighth century) said, "God has collected the sciences of earlier revelatory Books in the Qur'an; then he collected the sciences of the Qur'an in the 'Opening'. Whoever knows what this means has acquired the meaning of the whole Book".

It is worth looking in detail at the text of this sura:

1. *Bismi' llàhi' r-rahmàni' r-rahìm(i)*
   In the name of God, the most gracious, the merciful
2. *Al-hàmduli' llàhi ràbbi' l- 'àlamìn(a)*
   Praise be to God, Lord of the worlds
3. *ar-rahmàni' r-rahìm(i)*
   The most gracious, the merciful
4. *màliki yàwmi' d-dìn(i)*
   Lord of the Day of Judgement
5. *iyyàka nà' budu wa iyyàka nastaìn(u)*
   We worship You and call on You for assistance
6. *ìhdina' s-siràta' l-mustaqìm(a)*
   Show us the right way
7. *siràtà' lladhìna an' àmta 'alàyhim ghàyri' l-maghdùbi 'alàyhim wa là' d-dallìn(a)*
   the way of those on whom you have granted your grace, not of those with whom you are angry and those who have turned away from the right path

The first and third verse, according to some Muslim scholars, reveal the essence of God; the second and fourth, his omnipotence. The last three are about humanity and reveal the secret of the connection between humanity and God. So in the "Opening" we find all the pillars of faith collected together: knowledge of God, and knowledge of what we owe to God.

The sura of "Unity" or of "Sincere Worship" (112) enunciates absolute monotheism and represents—according to al-Ghazali, who seems to reproduce a prophetic tradition—a third of the Qur'an:

Bismi' llàhi' r-rahmàni' r-rahìm(i)
1. *Qùl huwa' llahu àhad(un)*
2. *Allàhu' s-sàmad(u)*
3. *Làm yàlid wa lam yùlad*
4. *Wa làm yàkun làhu kufu 'àn àhad(un)*

In the name of God, the Most Gracious, the Merciful

1. Say: God, He is One
2. God is eternal
3. He does not beget, and nor was he begotten
4. And there are none like Him

The chapter concentrates on the essence of God. His Unity is affirmed in the first verse. The second, which is variously interpreted depending upon how one understands the Arabic term *samad*, suggests that He is beyond human consciousness and his existence is outside time or that He is the protector of human beings who must address to Him their prayers. Actually, *samad* has many possible meanings (as I will discuss in Chapter 3 in this volume, wherein a thorough theological analysis of the sura will be presented). The third verse is a key negation of the Christian idea that God had a son (Jesus). The fourth verse expresses transcendence.

A second example consists in the sura 81 (The Darkening). It is worth recalling that from the Muslim perspective all translations are completely unable to render the meaning of the holy Qur'an that in itself consists of words that came directly from God and is untranslatable. Every non-Arabic version of the text seems to be forced and artificial. All translation is, as we know, an interpretation. Here we give in parentheses the final Arabic words that come at the end of each verse to given an idea of the rhyme of the original.

The Darkening (81)
In the name of God the most Gracious, the Merciful

When the sun is folded up	(*kùwwirat*)
and the sky darkens	(*inkàdarat*)
and the mountains disappear	(*sùyyirat*)
and the pregnant camel looks after herself	('*ùttilat*)
and the wild beasts all come together	(*hùshirat*)
and the sea boils over	(*sùjjirat*)
and each soul comes together;	(*zùwwijat*)
and when a female being buried alive is questioned	(*sù'ilat*)
for what crime she was killed;	(*qùtilat*)
and when the holy Book is opened	(*nùshirat*)
and Heaven crashed down	(*kùshitat*)
and the burning fire is kindled	(*sù''irat*)

and Paradise is brought close	(*ùzlifat*)
then each soul will know what it has introduced.	(*àhdarat*)
I witness the planets	(*khùnnas*)
turning vessels,	(*kùnnas*)
through the night as it starts to fall	(*ʿàs ʿas*)
and the start of the day as it lights up!	(*tanàffas*)
And this is the word of a noble Messenger,	(*karìm*)
someone with power and status before He who	
sits on the Throne,	(*makìn*)
obedient and faithful.	(*amìn*)
Your companion is not someone who is mad,	(*majnùn*)
but has seen him on the clear horizon,	(*mubìn*)
He does not obstinately withhold the mystery	(*danìn*)
nor is it the expression of cursed Satan!	(*rajìm*)
Where do you go?	(*tadhhabùn*)
This is a warning for creation,	(*ʿalamìn*)
to whichever of you wishes to follow the	
recommended path.	(*yastaqìm*)
But you will not will except as God wishes,	
the Lord of creation!	(*ʿalamìn*)

The rapid rhythm, which is almost suffocating, the culminating vision of the terrible moment of the end of the world; the oaths and curses; the understanding that there is a supreme force, without any limits in its power, that governs the universe—everything demonstrates, especially in the riming original Arabic, that the Arabic structure of the original text gives this chapter a literary character of great potency, something that the translation cannot hope to reproduce fairly.

Equally effective from the literary point of view is sura 100, which is worth a brief formal study. The chapter is clearly divided into three parts, organized by a distinct rhythm. We will show the transliteration of the Arabic, a translation by Arberry (A) and a more literal translation by myself (L) rendered in English:

Bismiʾllàhiʾr-rahmàniʾr-rahìm(i)
In the name of God, the Most Gracious, the Merciful

1. *Waʾl-ʿadiyàt dàbhan*
   (A) By the snorting chargers
   (L) By the galloping panting [referring to horses]

2. *Fa'l-muriyàt qàdhan*
   (A) By the strikers of fire
   (L) by that which sparks fire
3. *Fa'l-mughiràt sùbhan*
   (A) By the dawn-riders
   (L) by that which made inroads in the morning
4. *Fa-athàrna bìhi nàq'an*
   (A) Blazing a trail of dust
   (L) producing in this way [clouds of] dust
5. *Fa-wasàtna bìhi jàm'an*
   (A) Cleaving there with a host
   (L) finding themselves in this way in the heap
6. *Inna'l-insàna li-ràbbihi la-kanùd(un)*
   (A) Surely man is ungrateful to his Lord
   (L) really, man is ungrateful to his Lord
7. *Wa ìnnahu 'àla dhàlika la-shahìd(un)*
   (A) And surely he [man] is a witness against that
   (L) and he of this is witness [this could mean, as some suggest, God]
8. *Wa ìnnahu li-hùbbi'l-khàyri la-shadìd(un)*
   (A) Surely he [always the man] is passionate in his love for good things
   (L) and he loves strongly the good [of this world? Then it means man, but the subject otherwise could be God]
9. *A-fa-là yà 'lamu ìdha bù 'thira mà fi'l-qubùr(i)*
   (A) Knows he not that when that which is in the tombs is overthrown
   (L) but does he not know [that] when everything will be turned upside-down that was found in the tombs
10. *Wa hùssila mà fi's-sudùr(i)*
    (A) And that which is in the breasts is brought out
    (L) when will be seen outside what is in the chests [hearts]
11. *Inna ràbbahum bìhim yaùma'ìd-dìnin la-khabìr(un)*
    (A) Surely on that day their Lord shall be aware of them!
    (L) truly which day your Lord is knowledgeable [will know] about them

The first part of the sura comprises the verses 1–5. It describes a cavalry attack, perhaps during a raid, in which the riders bring confusion in the ranks of the enemy. The image is used to introduce the second part, the verses 6–8. The divine voice warns, through the potent image of war, that humanity is not grateful to God and is too attached to the world, and it calls on him to acknowledge his sinfulness. (But perhaps we should say that God Himself, loving the good, knows the evil that men carry out, and everything depends on the interpretation of the subject "he".) In the third part (9–11) we are told that God knows what is locked up in human hearts and in graves, and will take account of this on the day of judgment. The meaning of the chapter is obviously eschatological, and its moral is illustrated through a common experience in Bedouin life, that of a raid and an improvised assault.

Not all the chapters of the Qur'an require rendering into a rhythmical or at least poetic form in a Western language. The Medinan suras especially contain some very long verses dealing with normative issues, such as that of heredity (4.11–12) or on debts and being a witness (2.282). We cannot straightforwardly interpret in Western idiom a language that uses verbal assonance or other poetic artifices. It is useful to look at verse 2.282 in which several forms of the root *shhd* appear, meaning witness (as far as faith is concerned, while *shahid* means also martyr):

> O you who believe, when you contract a debt for a certain term, write it down, and let a scribe write it down for you correctly, and let him not refuse to do what God has taught him. Let him write and let the debtor dictate it. Let him fear God his Lord, and not diminish anything that he owes. If the debtor is stupid or weak [in mind] or unable to dictate, then let his guardian dictate rightly. Call in to witness (*wa 'stashhidu*) two witnesses (*shahidayn*), out of your men or if the two are not men, then one man and two women, who you choose as witnesses (*shuhada'*) so that if one of them goes wrong, the other can remind her. The witnesses should not refuse when they are called upon. Do not be reluctant to write it [the debt] down whether it is large or small, it is more just in the sight of God and more justifiable for testimony (*shahada*) and more likely that you will not doubt. In the case of goods that are present there is no blame on you if you do not write it down. Take witnesses (*ashhidu*) when you make a contract and let neither the writer nor the witness suffer. If you do, it would be a great sin.

In any case, some of these techniques and forms of representation in the previous quoted sura 81 are repeated often in Qur'anic chapters and confer on the text its unique literary character. For example the terrible evocation of the end of the world is a common theme of the Meccan period. We could cite many other passages, but we will limit ourselves here to sura 101 in the translation of Arberry that puts in poetic mode the terrible warning of the Prophet of the imminence of the final Hour:

> In the name of God, the Merciful, the Compassionate
> the Clatterer (*al-qari'a*)
> What is the Clatterer?
> And what shall teach thee what is the Clatterer?
> The day that men shall be like scattered moths,
> and the mountains shall be like plucked wool-tufts.
>
> Then he whose deeds weigh heavy in the Balance
> shall inherit a pleasing life.
> but he whose deeds weigh light in the Balance
> shall plunge in the womb of the Pit
> And what shall teach thee what is the Pit?
> A blazing Fire!

The oaths and curses confer a character and dramatic tone on the text. Sura 111 expresses the profound disagreement of Muhammad in his confrontation with one of his most bitter enemies, Abu Lahab, a Meccan who was energetically opposed to Islam: "Perish the hands of the Father of Flame (Abu Lahab) and let there be no profit to him from all his wealth and gain. He will soon be burnt in a fierce fire and his wife, the carrier of wood, will be the fuel, with a twisted rope of palm-leaf fiber round [her] neck".

Sura 114 is often used as an amulet or talisman against the evil eye and other troubles. The very brief chapter has an urgent scansion, and it is worth yet again reproducing the transliteration of the Arabic text in order to demonstrate its rhythmical efficacy (the "s" in the rhyme is hard as in "assassin", not sibilant as in "snake").

Bismi 'llàhi 'r-rahmàni 'r-rahìm(i)
In the name of God, the Most Gracious, the Merciful

1. *Qùl a'ùdhu bi-ràbbi 'n-nàs(i)*
    Say: I seek refuge with the Lord of men

2. *Màliki 'n-nàs(i)*
    The King of men
3. *Ilàhi 'n-nàs(i)*
    The God of men
4. *Min shàrri 'l-waswàsi 'l-khannàs(i)*
    From the evil of the whisperer who gives up
5. *Allàdhi yuwàswis fi sudùri 'n-nàs(i)*
    From him who whispers into the hearts of men
6. *Min al-jìnnati wa 'n-nàs(i)*
    of jinn and men

Some famous exponents of Islam from its original period, like the Companion Ibn Mas'ud, have maintained that sura 114 is spurious and an interpolation into the Qur'an from later. The idea is that a sacred Book, the direct word of God, cannot contain profane subject matter and certainly not anything to do with magic, something strongly condemned and warned against in the Islamic tradition.

Sometimes the Qur'an uses repetitive expressions as a refrain. The most beautiful example is in sura 55 (Merciful), verses 10–77 from which this passage comes, and again the rendering of Arberry has been used in what follows:

[God] created man of a clay like the potter's
and He created the jinn of a smokeless fire.
O which of your Lord's bounties will you and you deny?
Bi-ayy ala'ai rabbikuma tukadhdhibani
Lord of the Two Easts, Lord of the Two Wests.
O which of your Lord's bounties will you and you deny?
Bi-ayy ala'ai rabbikuma tukadhdhibani
He let forth the two seas that meet together.
Between them a barrier they do not overpass.
O which of your Lord's bounties will you and you deny?
Bi-ayy ala'ai rabbikuma tukadhdhibani
From them come forth the pearl and the coral.
O which of your Lord's bounties will you and you deny?
Bi-ayy ala'ai rabbikuma tukadhdhibani
His too are the ships that run, raised up in the sea like land-marks.
O which of your Lord's bounties will you and you deny?
Bi-ayy ala'ai rabbikuma tukadhdhibani

The Qur'an can be seen as an inexhaustible source of structural and linguistic analytical distinctions. This brings us to the topic of inimitability.

THE INIMITABILITY OF THE QUR'AN

The literary character of the structure of the Qur'an and the uniqueness of its magnificent language have suggested to Muslims that the text is "inimitable", and the inimitability of the Qur'an has become a theological principle in its own right. Indeed, the Qur'an itself affirms in many places its unique character. No human can produce anything better (10.38). Not even a combined effort of humans and demons could succeed in producing anything similar (17.88). The "canonical" doctrine of the inimitability of the Qur'an in Islamic theology is probably that of the Ash'arite jurist Abu Bakr al-Baqillani (d. 1013), which is a mixture of quotations and poetic selections. The Qur'anic language has an unusual character and distinguishes itself from the devices of poets since its source is taken to be divine. It is important to underline the artistic value, but not something supposed to be "poetic", of the Qur'an, and the Book says many times that Muhammad is not a poet (21.5; 36.69) but someone in receipt of inspiration. It also says many times that he is not a magician or bewitched (10.2; 11.7; and so on). The inimitability of the Qur'an brings divine inspiration to a level of exquisite literary sensibility and yet rescues it from the "poetry" of human beings and the ravings of charlatans. Inimitability really refers to literary quality but is not limited to it.

The debate on this topic developed during the course of Islamic thought. An "ultrarationalist" like the Mu'tazilite al-Nazzam (ninth century) proposed a demanding thesis—that the Qur'an is inimitable with respect to its Arabic language because God brought about a miracle by preventing human beings from producing anything similar, but not in the sense that this would involve having a divine understanding in order to produce a divine revelation. If it were not for God's forbidding humanity to try to copy Him, we could produce something even superior to the Qur'an in style. The superiority of the Book consists then in its content, not in its form. Al-Nazzam's thesis produced other suggestions on this topic that are not necessary to consider here. It is enough to note that in reaction to this

Mu'tazilite idea Abu Bakr al-Baqillani underlined the unique character of the Qur'an as residing in the fact that it is neither prose nor poetry, but a literary genre of its own. Inimitability is taken to be expressed in three ways. "The first relates to information about the invisible (*gha'ib*), since there is no way that human beings have the ability to acquire this level of knowledge. The second is as has been noted that the Prophet was illiterate and could neither read nor write. It follows that he had no understanding or knowledge of earlier books, their reports, their history, biography or anything at all about them. Despite this, he reported on future events in history, on past events and on the creation of Adam and the accounts that are related to it. He talked about Noah, Abraham, and all the other prophets mentioned in the Qur'an. The Prophet had no way of knowing about these things, unless he received them through divine illumination. The third feature is that the Qur'an is wonderfully organized and composed, there is something sublime in its literary elegance which makes it accessible by everyone" (quoted in Abu Zayd 2003).

The modern Egyptian thinker Kamil Husayn has written on the inimitability of the Qur'an and says it consists of three things: "The Qur'an is a guide for human beings from both a spiritual and a temporal point of view. From the perspective of human psychology, inimitability appears in the force of its style and sound and its ability to affect human thinking deeply as well as to encourage and develop the noble feelings of humanity. Inimitability is placed on the level of the purely literal due to the power of Qur'anic style. The Qur'an produces a deep impression in all sorts of people who have even a tiny amount of sensibility for Arabic" (quoted in PISAI 1985: 137–139). The inimitability of the Qur'an also consists in the fact that it contains intimations of the future and hidden scientific facts that modern science has come to understand little by little. So the obscure allusion in 30.2–4 ("The Romans have been overcome, close to our land, but they will triumph after this defeat") refers to the struggles between the Byzantine Empire and the Persian Empire in the first decades of the seventh century (something that, as Bausani notes, demonstrates the antiquity of the verse). Verses like 22.5 and 23.12–14 apparently describe the process of conception and development of the embryo on its route to becoming a fully fledged human being, anticipating modern biological science: "O men, if you are in doubt about the resurrection . . . think about how We created you out of earth, then made you out of this earth and a clot of sperm, then a bit of adhesion, then a bit of flesh both formed and unformed, so that we could demonstrate Our power to you. According to Our will we let some rest in the maternal womb for an appointed term and then we bring you out in the form of a baby". Chapter 105 recounts how God miraculously broke up an attempted invasion of Arabia by bombarding the invaders with "hard stones". This reference to projectiles has been interpreted by the modernist al-Kawakibi (d. 1902) as an allusion to microbes and the viral diffusion of epidemics. These examples can be multiplied. Of course, such a strategy may seem to be apologetic or far-fetched in the ways they apparently stretch the text. They are evidence of the tendency of many Muslims to see the sacred Book as the source of all knowledge. We shall discuss this issue in Chapter 5 in this volume. For the moment the important thing is to appreciate that the question of inimitability lies at the heart of the positive attitude that Muslims have for their Book and is a universally accepted theological doctrine.

SUMMARY

In this chapter we have dealt with

- The history of the composition of the Qur'anic text as the Muslims narrate it.
- The orientalist critique of the Qur'anic language.
- The structure of the Qur'anic text, its articulations and the phases (Meccan and Medinan) of revelation.
- The literary character of the text, examining the issues of rhyme, style, translation and inimitability.

REFERENCES/READINGS

Abdul-Rauf, H. *Qur'an Translation: Discourse, Texture and Exegesis*, Curzon, Richmond 2001.

Abu Zayd, N.H. *Le Dilemme de l'Approche Littéraire du Coran*, cit. in www.etudes-musulmanes.com/textes, downloaded February 2003.

Arkoun, M. *Lectures du Coran*, Maisonneuve, Paris 1982.

Bausani, A. *Il Corano*, Rizzoli, Milano 1988.

Blachère, R. *Introduction au Coran*, Maisonneuve, Paris 1977.

Boullata, I.J. (a cura di), *Literary Structures of Religious Meaning in the Qur'ân*, Curzon, Richmond 2000.

Bucaille, M. *La Bible, le Coran et la Science*, Seghers, Paris 1976.

Campanini, M. "Qur'an and Science: A Hermeneutical Approach", *Journal of Qur'anic Studies* VII (1), 2005, pp. 48–63.

Luxenberg, C. *Die Syro-Aramäische Lesart des Korans: Ein Beitrege zur Entsschlusselung der Koransprache*, Verlag Hans Schiler, Berlin 2000.

PISAI (Pontifical Institute of Arabic and Islamic Studies), *Le Commentaire Coranique Contemporain*. Deuxième Partie: Le Tafsîr Moderne et Contemporain, Dossier des Etudes Arabes, n. 69, 1985.

Qutb, Sayyid *Al-Taswir al-fanni fi'l-Qur'an [The Artistic Imagination in the Qur'an]*, Dar al-Ma'arif, Cairo 1966.

Reynolds, G.S. *The Qur'an and Its Biblical Subtext*, Routledge, London-New York 2010.

Rippin, A. (ed.), *The Qur'an: Style and Contents*, Aldershot, Ashgate 2001.

Sadeghi, B. and Bergmann, U. "The Codex of a Companion of the Prophet and the Qur'an of the Prophet", *Arabica* 57 (4), 2010, pp. 343–436.

Sadeghi, B. and Goudarzi, M. "San'a1 and the Origins of the Qur'an", *Der Islam* 87 (1–2), 2012, pp. 1–129.

al-Salih, S. *Mabahith fi 'ulum al-Qur'an (Researches on the Qur'anic Sciences)*, Dar al-Mallaiyyn, Beirut 2002.

Sourdel, D. and Sourdel-Thomine, J. *La Civilisation de l'Islam Classique*, Arthaud, Paris 1968.

Watt, W.M. *Muhammad, Prophet and Statesman*, Oxford University Press, London-Oxford-New York 1974.

Watt, W.M. and Bell, R. *Introduction to the Qur'an*, Edinburgh University Press, Edinburgh 1970.

Welch, A.T. "Kor'ân," in *Encyclopedia of Islam,* Brill, Leiden, 1961.

3

GOD, HUMANITY AND PROPHECY

THE COHERENCE OF THE QUR'AN

An analysis, albeit not exhaustive, of the fundamental themes of the Qur'an is indispensable. On the one hand it is important to describe the content of the text, which, however immutable it might be in its written expression, can be the source of varying interpretations. On the other hand, it is important to restore the religious meaning of the Book while a few orientalists, like Michael Cook, pay little attention to its religious dimension.

It is perhaps possible to say that as in all fundamental books of a monotheistic religion, the basic themes of the Qur'an are both theological and anthropological. God has created humanity and revealed the Scripture for it. Humans are like God and in a sense descend from Him. The relationship between the transcendence of God and the immanence of the human world is guaranteed by prophecy. Treating these themes is representative of the religious content of the Qur'an and its complexity. However, as al-Ghazali said, the Qur'an is a "deep sea" that can never be exhausted. It is not possible to render the richness of the text in a few pages, and many important features have been put to one side here. An example is its scientific and cosmological dimensions, and it is impossible to linger on the historical accounts, not to mention the linguistic, ethnographic and so on that placed it at the heart of Arabic culture.

To reconstruct the thematic course of the Qur'an seems to be a difficult or rather impossible task. On one reading the text seems to be unsystematic, if not chaotic. Many suras, and especially the longer suras and those nearer us in time, contain a variety of themes that go into theological digressions into prophetic stories, moral advice and warnings about behavior. One of the premier twentieth-century Arabists, Francesco Gabrieli, defined the Qur'an as an "impossible muddle" (Gabrieli 1967: 65). The impression of Gabrieli is unjustified and is perhaps based on a rather superficial reading. Naturally, the shorter suras, the last in the organization of the text in terms of length, are very compact and deal with just one theme or even just one fact. The only chapter of a reasonable size that deals with one narrative is 12 (Joseph). Much briefer is sura 71 on Noah. But a sura like 2 (The Cow) contains a lot of arguments in a style that a Western reader cannot help thinking are disorganized. The reader who comes to the text for the first time, and is not a specialist, can often read it and find a lot in it, however. It is a good idea to read the shortest suras first—those that are stylistically more effective and closer to us in mood, those that appear at the end of the Book—and then tackle the more complex.

Despite this suggestion, we need to make some observations that may temper or even go against first impressions. In the first place, the disorder in the composition can be looked on as a demonstration of the authenticity of the text. It is likely that, if the text is "made up" from bits and pieces as some orientalists (see the next chapters in this volume) suggest, it would have been put together in a different and better way by first generations of Muslims. Whatever we can regard as the success of seeing the Hebrew Bible as the product of development over the centuries, and despite the incoherence in the text, there exists in the end a logically organized text. In the second place, the criteria of organization and of whether a text is chaotic or systematic are not exactly the same for an Arabic/Semitic sensibility as they are within contemporary Western culture. The Qur'an may represent well Arabic taste in a refined and precise manner that entirely escapes the Western reader. Commentators such as al-Mawdudi and Sayyid Qutb (see Chapter 5 in this volume) have strongly argued that sura 2 in its relationship with the others, and indeed all the Qur'anic chapters, follows a systematic plan, a very precise plan, of revelation. This argument has been accepted by just as many Muslims as Westerners. In the 2003 Conference on the Qur'an at the London School of Oriental and African Studies, Issa Boullata spoke of sura 30 (The Byzantines) as structured around the promises that God made to all human beings, and on how those promises are absolutely true and will invariably be realized. Neal Robinson referred to sura 3 (Family of 'Imran) and remarked on how this long chapter seemed to consist of diverse remarks that prevented it from being seen as clear. However, the chapter consists of revelations from different periods and represents a many-faceted approach to a unique and fundamental problem, the threat of renouncing Islam in the initial Muslim community. Anthony Johns is another scholar who has often suggested that it is possible to reconstitute the religious meaning of the text. The Qur'an is certainly a religious text of profound spiritual inspiration. Any account of its structure should reflect the religious significance of the text.

More recently Raymond Farrin (2014) demonstrated that the sura 2 (The Cow) is arranged according to a concentric pattern. The forerunner has been probably Michael Cuypers, who studied and systematically reconstructed the rationale of sura 5 (Cuypers 2007). The idea is that Qur'anic suras are composed and structured in accordance with the rules of Semitic and Arab rhetoric and literary style, far different from Western ones. Hasan Hanafi pointed to the classical concept of *nazm* referring to al-Jurjani's literary theory, while Ahmad al-Islahi (see Mir 1986), according to the principle of *nazm*, made a gigantic effort—not always successful in my view—to discover the internal coherence of the Qur'an on three levels: of the single sura; of the pairs of suras; of the groups of suras.

To sum up, nowadays Gabrieli's underevaluation of the Qur'an as an "impossible muddle" sounds to be a orientalist prejudice.

CONCEPTIONS OF GOD: HIS ESSENCE

The Qur'an is committed to an absolute monotheism. The whole Book is full of expressions and verses that deal with this fundamental doctrine in Islam. It is useful to repeat the very brief sura "On Unity" or "Sincere Worship" that defines the notion of *tawhid* or unity:

1.   Say:
2.   He, God,

3.   is One
4.   God is *samad*
5.   He does not beget, and nor was he begotten
6.   And there is nothing like him

Al-Ghazali in the *Pearls of the Qur'an* stated that, with its role in defining the essence of God and his unity, sura 112 constitutes a "third" of the Qur'an (the other two thirds being the knowledge of the Last Day and the right Way—in other words, eschatology and anthropology).

Thus I believe interesting a thorough study of the *sura* word by word.

1.   The command to speak ("Say . . .") is obviously addressed to the Prophet Muhammad, who is simply the transmitter of the divine message; he is "inspired" by God but repeats *verbatim* what he hears. However, it is not clear who utters the command. Is the speaker God Himself or the Angel (Gabriel)? The answer to the question is not important in itself. What is important is that the message is the literal and straightforward speech/word of God. Moreover the following of divine Oneness is an imperative prescription cannot be questioned.
2.   The Prophet is commanded to proclaim that *Huwa Allah* (He, God) . . . is One. The word "Huwa" has a metaphysical meaning, because one of the most important theological pillars of Islam is the divine "ipseity", *huwwiyya* in Arabic, deriving from "huwa". Ipseity or *huwwiyya* means that God is Himself and no other thing can be like Him. Al-Ghazali helps us to understand this peculiarity in a very pregnant phrase: "In the sentence *la ilah illa huwa* [there is no god but Him], *al-ilah* [God] does mean that He is the Deity, while *illa huwa* [(no god) but Him] means that "as there is no god but Him, there is no He but He" [*kama la ilah illa huwa la huwa illa huwa*]" (al-Ghazali 1986: 144). Thus, ipseity sounds very similar to the biblical "*Ego sum qui sum*", "I am who I am" (Es. 3,14).
3.   God is *ahad*, "one", and the Oneness of God consists both in Unity and in Uniqueness. God is One in numerical sense (He is not "two" or "three") and in metaphysical sense (He is a *unicum* so to speak in relation to the other beings). A Qur'anic

verse (Q. 21.22) states, "If there had been in the heavens and the earth a god (*ilah*) besides God (*allah*), indeed both [heavens and earth] would have ruined", because two gods would be in contradiction each other.

4. God is *samad*, and this attribute is one of the most controversial of the "Beautiful Names" referred to Him. Thus, it has been variously interpreted: Arberry has "Everlasting Refuge" , Dawood and Zilio Grandi "Eternal", Denise Masson "Impenetrable", etc. Al-Ghazali in the *Maqsad al-asna* interprets *samad* as "[t]he one whom one turns in need and the one who is intended in our desires" (al-Ghazali 1995: p. 131). *Samad* expresses the ineffability of God's essence.

5. The statement *He does not beget, and nor was he begotten* alludes in the first part, denying it, to the Christian principle that God "begot" a son Jesus, and in the second part to God's eternity, *a parte ante* and *a parte post*.

6. Finally, God is qualitatively different from any other thing: there is no ontological compromise between the Creator and the creatures. Another very important verse, much quoted by theologians, is 42.11: "Nothing is similar to Him" (*laysa ka-mithlihi shayy'un*), emphasizing God's transcendence.

A second verse of great significance in the theological structure of the sacred Text is the so-called "Throne Verse" (2.255) that, apart from proclaiming his Unity-Ipseity (*Allah la ilah illa huwa*), emphasizes divine omnipotence: "God, there is no God except Him, the Living, the Self-Sufficient. Neither slumber nor sleep can affect him. To him belongs everything in the heavens and on Earth. Who can intercede before Him without his permission? He knows what is before [humanity] and after and behind. They do not understand anything about Him except what He wills. His Throne stretches over the heavens and the Earth, and he has no difficulty in preserving them. He is the Highest, the Majestic". Al-Ghazali gives this passage a metaphorical meaning. After the affirmation of the Unity of God's being, the Living and Self-Sufficient indicate his attributes. He transcends the reality that is an effect of his omnipotence and omniscience. The Throne indicates the immensity of the divine Kingdom, and the perfection of his power, but under the veil of the words lies a secret that draws the attention of the lively intuition of the mystics.

The Qur'an "proves", as it were, the Unity of God in the verse 21.22: "If there were in them [the heaven and the Earth] a[n] [other] god like God, they would cancel each other out" because two gods would act in opposite ways and the world would be destroyed. A philosopher like al-Farabi (c. 870–950) seems to move the Qur'anic allusion to the rational level of philosophy when he claims, in his *Virtuous City*, that God cannot have anyone standing against him since, if there were two gods, they would finish each other off, since they would each be open to decay, and also because they would destroy each other.

Divine Unity is also discussed in some allegorical verses, whose interpretation is quite varied (we will talk about the "ambiguous" verses in the Qur'an in detail in Chapter 4 in this volume). The most fascinating of these verses seems to me to be 57.3: "God is the First and the Last, the Manifest and the Hidden. He is of all things knowledgeable". God is the alpha and the omega of reality, but his presence is hidden. Al-Ghazali said that God is absolutely obvious "in every little thing in the heavens and the Earth, in the planets and the stars, the Sun, the Moon, animals and plants, in attributes or substance, everything provides evidence through the very fact of its existence that there has to be a Being that came before it" (al-Ghazali 1987:137) .

There is nothing like Him (42.11): the verse repeats the absolute singularity of God from 112, and that it is stated in a number of different ways seems to the theologians to confirm His transcendence. To God belongs the most beautiful "names" (7.180; 20.8; and other verses), and particularly significant to the issue is 59.22–24: "He (huwa) is God, there is no other than Him (*la ilah illa huwa*), who knows the visible and the invisible, the Merciful, the Gracious. He is God, there is no other than Him, the King, the Holy One, the Pacific, the Faithful, the Guardian, the Preserver, the Powerful, the Invincible, the Supreme. Glory to God, who is above what is said about Him. He is God, the Creator, the Producer, the Former, these are his Beautiful Names, and whatever is in the heavens and on the Earth sings his praises. He is the Mighty, the Wise". Thus the names of God are developed in an intense activity of symbolic unveiling with mystical and philosophical features, which impressed al-Ghazali and such theologians as Fakhr al-Din al-Razi (twelve century) and the Egyptian Sufi mystics Ibn 'Ata' Allah (thirteenth century). The ninety-nine names that the theologians and popular piety attribute to God come from the Qur'an, with a hundredth name that is secret and known only to the deity.

It would be useful to look at a philosophical interpretation of some of the names by al-Ghazali. For example, he comments on the expressions *zahir* (manifest) and *batin* (hidden) thus:

The Manifest, the Hidden. The two labels can be seen to be complementary since the Clear is only a matter of degree, as is the Hidden. Something cannot be clear and hidden at the same time, but on the other hand it could be clear from one perspective and hidden from another. The obvious and the hidden are present in everything visible, and the High God has hidden himself in order to be approached through the perceptions of the senses and the force of imagination, and he has made it clear that he might be investigated applying the resources of the intellect through inductive reasoning. It might be objected "That God is hidden from sensory perception is obvious, but that he is clear to the intellect, which is an obscure fact, is itself clear and not something about which there is doubt, and on which everyone is in agreement, but in the case of the manifestation of God people have many doubts. Is He then open?" and you should reply "Know that He is secret in spite of being open, since his openness is too powerful for us. This is the reason for his hiddenness, His light and the veil of his light".

(al-Ghazali 1987: 136)

The truth and the reality of God are thus so luminous that they are hidden in the shadows for contingent beings. Creatures are generally "signs" of God; they exist, but their existence, what we understand through our senses, "conceals" the existence of God, which can be appreciated only through the intellect. The intellect has the capacity to assess the "light" of God from the "darkness" of physical existence, grasping the halo that, from the luminous source, through the contours of the body, is reflected between it and the eye.

Al-Ghazali theorizes further on the absolute rationality of the cosmic order, that this time belongs to a divine attribute:

The Judge (*al-hakam*). He is someone who judges and decrees; the magistrate who cannot be argued with, whose judgement (*hukm*) cannot be resisted and whose decree cannot be changed. [. . .] If the meaning of rulership ([wisdom] *hikma*) is the organization of causes

and their application to what is caused, God can be defined in an absolute sense as the "Judge" because He is the one who causes all causes,
as much in general as in particular. From the Judge we derive the decree
and divine predestination (*qada wa'l-qadar*). The [divine] organization
is the principle that grounds the cause, so that the judge [determina-
tion] and God's decree can apply itself to the cause. He has brought
about the universal, original, constant and continuing causes, that cannot stop nor be changed—like the Earth, the seven heavens, the stars,
planets, and their coordinated and constant movements that cannot
be modified or negated—as has been written until it comes to its final
end. Such is the decree of God, for He has said "He created seven heavens in two days and each heaven has been given its orders" (41.12).
God has directed the causes, their harmonious second movements,
so that they are fixed, smooth, organized, and so that they can bring
about what they are supposed to cause. Such is its predestination. This
is a reference to the "decree" and the first universal organization, the
eternal order that [is created] in a fluttering of the eye (see 16.77). The
decree is the global position of continuing and fixed causes. Predestination is the directing of universal causes through their movement
impressing themselves on what they bring about. They are calculated
and defined according to an order that does not suffer any increment
or diminution.

(al-Ghazali 1987: 92f.)

The causal structure of the world is justified from the point of view
of quality and the divine attributes, especially when we consider the
creative capacity of God:

The Creator (*al-Khaliq*), the Producer (*al-Bari'*), the Former (*al-Musawwir*).
You should think about what these names are equivalent to and that they
all come down to the act of creating and "finding out". However, it is not
necessary that things are like this, for everything that has moved from
non-existence to existence has in the first place been produced, and in the
second has been made to exist, according to a preceding process, and in
the third place after having been made to exist, it is shaped. Hear, God,
praise is due to You the Highest, you are the Creator of great processes,
Producer through your transformation of material into existence and Mod-
eller through working on organizing new forms in the best way possible.

[. . .]

> In this respect the name of the Modeller belongs to God through his orga-
> nizing the forms of things according to the best order and in the best way.
>
> (al-Ghazali 1987: 75ff.)

God is actively involved in the construction and preservation of the world. In any case, He remains above everything and beyond time and space. "Nothing lasts except his Face" (28.88; 55.27). And the Face of God, as al-Ghazali and Ibn 'Arabi (1165–1240) have interpreted it, is that totality of being and authentic existence that remains beyond the ephemeral and the transient nature of inauthentic mundane existence. God knows the visible and the invisible "and from whom nothing is hidden, not even the weight of an atom in the heaven and on Earth" (34.3).

The chief esoteric verse—especially for the commentators, philosophers or otherwise—is that of Light: "God is the Light of the heavens and the Earth, and His light resembles a Niche in which there is a Lamp, and the Lamp is in a Glass and the Glass is like a radiant Star, and the Lamp is lit with the oil from an olive, a blessed tree, neither from the East nor from the West, whose oil sparkles although untouched by fire. Light upon Light" (24.35; this English translation is based on the Italian of Bausani that seems to be particularly efficacious in representing the Arabic original).

It would be interesting to look briefly at some of the ways in which verse 24.35 has been interpreted, in medieval theology. Some Shiite theologians have suggested that the niche points to Fatima, wife of 'Ali, while the Light represents Husayn, son of 'Ali, and the expression "Light upon Light" alludes to the succession of imams, the relatives of 'Ali who have received his spiritual heritage. An Isma'ili thinker like Abu Ya'qub al-Sijistani has seen in the verse the symbolization of metaphysical aspects of Shi'ite gnosis in particular referring to the succession of imams. The Light is not natural light, that which comes from the Sun, but the principle of reason stemming from the divine Word. It can be seen in terms of the cosmic pair of the Preceding (*sabiq*, "intellect" or "reason") or the Following (*tali*, "the soul"), a mystery and allusive concept quite typical of Isma'ili theology. The Lamp is the lamp of knowledge of Muhammad that he bestows on his Community at the end of guiding it with the Light of knowledge to God, freeing it of the darkness as a result of doubt and dissension. Al-Sijistani concludes that the glass refers to the first imam Hasan, son of 'Ali, whose imamate was fragile like a pane of glass. The star is Husayn, the second imam. The olive, the oil and the fire are the three imams who successively led to the sixth, Ja'far al-Sadiq. The philosopher Avicenna (980–1037) read in this verse the esoteric seal of the doctrine of the intellects. People are differentiated in terms of different levels of intellect, between the potential or material, the active, whether in habit or acquired. Now, the intellects contain each other (the crystal that contains the lamp that in its turn contains the niche), and everything comes to an end in the acquired intellect, where the perfection of the intelligible is reached, as in "Light upon Light". According to al-Ghazali, God is the "Light of the heaven and the Earth" in so far as all reality is gathered in him alone as far as the natural world is concerned. It is the illumination and visible explication of his Unity. The other symbols refer to the levels of the human "spirits" according to the gradations of the faculty of knowledge.

The metaphor of light recurs in other parts of the Qur'an. There is a reference to God opening someone's heart to Islam and as a result receiving God's light (39.22), and also that he who does not receive light from God will not have light (24.40). Light guides and sustains all in the true faith and is a gift of God yet not provided to those wandering in the darkness. According to Islam, in order to prevent obsessions, uncertainties and fears tormenting humanity, it is necessary to set out to seek the divine light.

CONCEPTIONS OF GOD: HIS ACTIONS

The previous is a summary of what the Qur'an has to say in allusion to the essence of God. God may be chiefly grasped through his actions. The first of God's actions is obviously creation. God creates and creates with the word ("When he has decreed a thing, he says only to it 'Be!' and it is"—*yaqul lahu kun fa-yakunu*" [2.117; 6.72; 40.68]). The idea of creation through the word is a common notion in the Near (or Middle) East. It is found in ancient Egypt, where the god Ptah produces the universe through intelligence and the word. In Babylon the power to create lies in the fiat that is a specific faculty of the god Marduk. It is found especially in the biblical book of Genesis, and also in St. John the Evangelist in terms of the Logos, the Verb or the Word. Christ was after all with God for all eternity. God has imposed on the universe his Order and the Order is based on his Spirit ("The spirit comes from the Order of my Lord" [see 17.85]). We could perhaps speculate that in organizing the world and everything that exists, God instills being with his Spirit, which organizes it and makes it come alive. In the verse 16.22 we find Order and Spirit taken as allusions to the process of revelation: "God's Command comes. . . . He sends the angels with his Spirit to bring his Command".

God is always involved in a new creation (21.104). Creation is not finished as a result of a final and conclusive process. God produces the universe and keeps on producing it (29.19). Creation starts off and keeps on being repeated (30.27). He is *al-khallaq*, a divine name that Bausani translates as "the Always-Creating" and Arberry "All-Creator", and everything is revived after its death (36.78–81). He is the inexhaustible regulator of the universe (we have already seen that he neither slumbers nor tires in carrying out this activity). However, he creates not haphazardly but according to a Truthful purpose (14.19; 20.16) and a providential and distinct plan. In the beginning there was some "primeval matter", labeled "smoke" from which God started the creative work (41.11), rather like the story in the Bible in the first chapter of Genesis. God has separated the primordial matter (21.30) and created out of it seven heavens, perfectly organized (67.3: "He who created seven heavens one above the other, You will not see any lack of proportion in the creation of the Most Gracious. Turn your eyes [upwards]. Do you see perhaps any flaw?"). You cannot see any irregularity or imprecision in the creation of the cosmos, since he formed and regulates the stars, and God orders the structure of the sky (10.5; 55.5). The heavens display the signs of God (51.7) and "will be rolled up in his right hand" (39.67). The creation of humanity is also evidence of a perfect plan (23.12–14).

The Qur'an underlines how the divine works are "rational", and the rationality of the construction constitutes an implicit invitation to everyone to exercise their rationality, thinking about the signs of God (3.190–191): "In the creation of the heavens and the earth and in the differentiation between night and day are signs for those who can think. Those who praise God whether sitting or lying down on their sides and thinking about the creation of the heavens and the Earth [saying] 'Our Lord, You have not created all this for nothing' ". There are many other verses that take a similar line like 13.2–4: "God is the one who has raised the heavens without visible pillars and sits on his Throne. He gives orders to the Sun and the Moon and each runs its course for a certain time. He is in charge of the Causes and understands every detail of the signs, so that you may believe with complete certainty one day that you will meet Him. And it is He who has laid out the Earth and set on it mountains that are immobile and rivers and fruit of every kind in pairs, and he wraps up the day as a veil over the night. There are certainly in this signs for those who can reflect (*yatafakkaruna*). And on the earth here are plots of land and gardens and cornfields and vineyards and corn and palms either by themselves or otherwise and watered by the same kind of water. Yet some of them we make more agreeable to eat than others. In this there are surely signs for those who can reason (*ya'qiluna*)". The questions calling for a rational response in the Qur'an are some of the main points of interest of contemporary investigation, as we shall see in Chapter 5 in this volume.

It is interesting to note that the evidence of the existence of God constitutes an example of this "rational" Qur'an. It is possible to analyze the shades of meaning that are involved in the term *haqq*. *Haqq* means both "truth" and "reality", and these meanings can be directly found in the Qur'an. *Haqq* is used more than two hundred times in the sacred Book. There are many verses linking God to the Truth or the True (*Allah huwa al-haqq*—for example, 10.32; 22.6; 24.25; etc.), and this means that God is reality in the sense that he is above everything and without limits. It is a renewed assertion of "ipseity" (*huwwiyya*): the Arabic locution *Allah huwa huwa* means "God is God or God is Himself". Al-Ghazali affirms that God is *haqq* since He is "[t]he Only Being who really exists in himself, in whom all real things find their authentic reality" (al-Ghazali 1987: 126). The verses 32–36 of sura 10 (Jonah) bring out to a degree four meanings of *haqq*. It is like a divine attribute, equivalent to "good" and opposite of "evil", as the ultimate end of human life in the notion of "God as the guide of all Truth", and from an epistemological point of view as an assertion of absolute wisdom, where the true is contrasted with what is merely possible opinion (*zann*). Against the danger of deviating from the right path, men know that the Qur'an is *haqq* (e.g., 2.144). Examples of verses that go against the truth (*haqq*) are those that are false and vain (*batil*), like: "We oppose the Truth to falsity so that the Truth (*haqq*) comes out on top and the false (*batil*) is wiped out". The pair of opposing terms *haqq* and *batil* comes to be used when referring to God: "God is the truth (*Allah huwa al-haqq*) and vanity (*batil*) is that which they associate with God" (31.30). In the already cited commentary by the two Jalals, we find the term *haqq* in 31.30 interpreted as "He who is permanent" and persists eternally. By contrast vanity is what miscreants worship in place of God and is "the ephemeral and the changeable". The existence of God is seen as absolutely obvious in connection with a world that is perishable and corruptible. God is the Truth, and he bears witness to the Truth as much in revelation as in the world that he has created and stands as the pure by contrast with the corruptible, the absolutely concrete with respect to the malleable.

QUR'ANIC ANTHROPOLOGY

The Qur'an reserves to humanity a post and a role that is quite remarkable. It is a characteristic peculiar to monotheisitic religions, very different from Hinduism or Buddhism, that privileges nature and its harmony with respect to the superiority of humans as the most important creatures and in the image of God. The high status of humanity in Islam is justified by the fact that humanity is the "caliph" or vicegerent of God on Earth (2.30; 38.26). Now, God has taught humans the names of everything, and this knowledge makes them superior to the angels. The origin of language, after all, according to most Muslim theologians is not natural but revealed. Humans have learnt language from God, but, as a result of having been preferred by God with respect to the angels in order to receive this sort of "revelation", humans are made perhaps a creature that is more perfect than the angels. Iblis, one of the angels closest to the Highest, refused to bow down to a mortal creature and became evil and Satan, the greatest enemy of humanity (2.31–34). This is the Qur'anic version of the biblical story of the rebellion of Lucifer. It is important to note that the name "Satan" has in Arabic a precise equivalent— *shaytan*—while it is highly probable that Iblis is a translation of the Greek *diabolos*. It is not necessarily the case that Iblis and Satan/ shaytan are exactly the same person. The refusal of Iblis, in any case, is interpreted by some mystics like al-Jili and al-Hallaj, in a very suggestive manner. This was really a supreme act of love and adoration of the One. Iblis refused it not so much because it involved loving humanity, but rather he objected to loving humanity and so fell into polytheism. The event brings out two peculiar aspects of Qur'anic monotheism, the inscrutable and irresistible will of God, who can impose on his creation an apparently blasphemous act that involves the adoration of humanity. The fact that each divine decision is generally "just" according to the justice of God is irreducible for each human, and no one can dare to determine how the divine decisions are to be assessed. However, it is true that Qur'anic human is a Promethean figure. The human is characterized very much in terms of alliance with God, a serious alliance to support, which is unbalanced and disproportionate in size: "We offered the Pledge (*amana*) to the heavens, to the Earth and to the mountains, but they refused to take it on, and were frightened of it. But man accepted it, and was indeed perverse and unaware [of any rule]" (33.72).

In its confrontation with God, is humanity free? The fact of having accepted the pledge suggests a positive reply. But the worrying problem of theodicy and human freedom of action persists in all the monotheist religions and so naturally also in Islam. On the one hand, it is an obvious principle that God is omnipotent. This omnipotence, as we have seen, shows itself through the medium of the organized and rational structure of the universe. In the ordering of things, whether cosmic or human, the will of God determines good and evil, and this will cannot be changed by humans. The Qur'an contains a pregnant and significant phrase: *wa kana amru'llah qadaran maqduran* or "the order (or decision) of God is a decree decreed" (33.38). That does not mean so much providence, as much as authority (*qahr*) applied to things and to their orientation. An analogous concept is expressed in some verses where we read that the "habit, tendency" (*sunna*) of God cannot be altered (33.62; 35.43; 48.23). The ways of operating of God cannot be changed because He is logical in his decisions about the direction of the universe just as he is about human life. The Qur'an in some places affirms absolute power in God from a rather contrary point of view: "We raise by [different] degrees whomsoever we will" (6.83). And also: "He cannot be taken to account for his acts, but they [humans] can be for theirs" (21.23) because "your Lord is full of wisdom" (6.83). In the face of such determination, what can humanity do? The Qur'an contains as many verses that refer to lack of power as those to human freedom. To quote only two together, it can be said that humanity can be punished or rewarded for what it has done consciously (99.7–8), and also that humanity is not the creator of its acts (37.96). We can find this dichotomy in the whole of the Qur'an. For example, 2.286 confirms that "it [the soul] gets what it has acquired (*kasabat*) and against it comes what it has acquired". But, "is there a creator other than God?" (35.3). Now, the Ash'arite theologians say that God creates the acts of humanity, but humanity receives them in the sense of acquiring them (*kasb*) and is therefore not responsible. God is always closer to us than our jugular vein (50.16), and he knows all the secrets of humans (58.7). It is difficult to avoid the impression that humanity can do little against the "decree" of God, which remains "just" since He is the master of his kingdom.

Salvation or punishment in the next life in proportion or relation to what humanity has done represents a very strong principle of Islam. The warning of the "last day" (*al-waqi'a*, title of sura 56, a Meccan sura) gives a "day of noise" (*al-qari'a*, title of another Meccan sura, sura 101, that has been quoted already) and points to an upheaval of the universe happening just before God will preside as judge of the living and the dead. This idea is present throughout the Qur'an, but in particular in the Meccan part of the Qur'an. In fact, we can recognize throughout the story of the revelation of Muhammad that two fundamental themes of the Meccan period (perhaps *the* two fundamental themes) are the exhortation for social justice and the warning of the imminence of the Last Day. Read the following verses, all Meccan, where the two aspects are brought together: "You are distracted [from God] in piling up [your riches] until you visit the graves. But you will soon know. Again, you will soon know!" (102.1–4); "Don't you see he who denies the Day of Judgment? He is someone who rejects the orphan and does not contribute to the feeding of the poor" (107.1–2). A bit later, at Medina, the need to organize the Community took up much of the social inspiration of the revelation and resulted in a less urgent and pressing eschatological anxiety.

POLITICS

A feature of great interest in Qur'anic anthropology is what gives us information about politics and social behavior (in Arabic *mu'amalat*). This is an aspect of great importance today and succeeded in shaking things up in religious terms also. The Qur'an constitutes, obviously, the foundation of such a project. After all, the sacred book explicitly sanctions the equality of humans wherever they are (and following this principle, there are no differences based on diversity or between men and women). At least two verses establish this equality. Verse 49.13 recognizes that all humans come from one source, and so cultural and political differences are a result of chance. This is evidence, like the color of skin, does not provide grounds for discrimination (the only appropriate discrimination is between believers and non-believers): "O men, we created man and woman, and we organized in terms of people and tribes in order that you should come to know each other. The noblest of you in the sight of God is the one who is more believer (than others)". The verse 10.19 repeats that humanity constitutes at heart a sole community and that only in subsequent times was it divided up by dissension: "Men made up just one community (*umma*) but divided up". In several other places the Qur'an affirms that all this was willed by God, in order to put to the test the moral solidity of his creatures.

The "political" verses of the Qur'an are few and more devoted to establish moral and ethical norms for guiding humanity than to organize a "state" or a "government". I think it is possible to distinguish, through a short analysis, those that involve teachings that prescribe the good and prohibit the evil, and those that deal with justice. The first are contained in 3.104 and 110: "You should constitute [meaning the Muslims] a Community (*umma*) urging the good, recommending what is right and forbidding what is wrong. These are the ones who prosper . . . you are the best Community, developed from humanity, pursuing what is right, forbidding the wrong and believing in God". The formula, coming directly from the sacred Book itself, of recommending the right and forbidding the wrong, constitutes a common theme of all Islamic theology and is agreed on as much by the Mu'tazilites as the Ash'arites and the Hanbalites. It implies that all Muslims have the duty of putting right or interfering in the wrongs that they witness—according to a *hadith*—with their hands, words or heart, through action, warning or prayers.

The key point here is that of "justice" ('*adl*). We find it in this claim that is central in verse 5.8: "O you who believe, stand up straight for God, as fair (*qist*) witnesses, and do not let those who hate you prevent you from doing the right thing. Act according to justice because this is the closest thing to piety". *Qist* is another word root that is linked with justice and can be translated as "the balance of equity". In many places the Qur'an uses the metaphor of balance to allude to justice. For example, in 57.25, the Balance (*mizan*) was revealed together with the Book (*kitab*) that was sent to humanity to encourage it to observe equity (*qist*). The idea of balance and of just measure is found in the concept of *'adl*, both from a legal and a moral point of view. Legally speaking, it is necessary to judge in accord with the right measure (*qist*; see 5.42) and to judge humans with justice (4.58; see below). The sacred Book does not explicitly connect the concept of judging and of justice in the courts. But in legal language *'adl* means the integrity and honesty of witnesses (or of judges and their sovereigns or caliphs) that ought to be just in the exercise of their court duty. The integrity of evidence is dealt with in 4.135, where people are warned to act justly in their dealings with their parents and relations. From the moral point of view, al-Ghazali underlines that "the meaning of justice (*'adl*) is to put everything in the right place" (al-Ghazali 1970: 105). As always with this theologian there is an agreement between the interior and the exterior. Justice is the straightening of the heart when it is used by the body to pursue the right rule. The world of conscience and the world of matter thus come together, and al-Ghazali interprets correctly the Qur'anic intent of 4.135: you should not follow the passions if you do not want to deviate from justice.

The problem of justice from a political and not moral perspective is raised with great precision in the so-called "Power" verse or *ayat al-umara'* (4.58–59): "God commands you to return your deposits to those who have a right to them, and when you judge between man and man, that you judge justly (*'adl*). [. . .] O you who believe, obey God, obey the Messenger [Muhammad] and those who have authority over you. If you disagree about anything put the issue to God and to his Messenger". The meaning of the verse is clear: the governors, those who "judge", ought to follow a strategy of justice. The governed have the duty to obey. This bilateralism between the directors and the directed is placed by Ibn Taymiyya at the base of *siyasa shar'iyya*, or politics according to religious law. However, Ibn Taymiyya, respected for his high authority by many other theologians, underlines particularly that obedience to the government is only owed if it follows the laws of God. Otherwise rebellion is allowed, even compulsory. Verse 4.59 seems to imply quietism. But the Qur'an discusses the details of the management of power. So for instance the believers work on consulting each other (42.38), and the old Bedouin principle of "democracy" is sanctioned by God on a transcendent plane. Consultation or *shura* is in fact one of the principles of the idealized Islamic state developed by contemporary radical Muslims, so that "permission is given to those who have been attacked [to fight] because they have suffered injustice" (22.39). The Qur'an seems to accept the legitimacy of fighting for the redressing of wrong. God stands unequivocally on the side of the oppressed, helping the weak, for "he will not change [his attitude] to a people until they change it themselves" (13.11).The oppressed will inherited the earth (28.5) because their liberation must occur *here* in this life. Humanity has to change in order to expect help that can change the conditions of its life. It is a matter of a "judgment" (*hukm*) of God, which belongs only to Him (6.57; 12.40) and is incapable of being influenced in one way or the other. It is characteristic of a "judgment" that it indicates "power" (also *hukm*, *hukuma* is the government and so on). Expressions like that at 5.49 ("judge between them in accordance with what God has revealed") have been used by radical theoreticians like Sayyid Qutb to support the necessity of an Islamization of the state. After all, if both the government and the power belong to God, then it is necessary that people rigorously apply in social reality the Laws of God and judge in accordance with His revelation. However, claiming to find in the Qur'an clear rules of government and political conduct is, at the best, wishful thinking and, at the worst, a distortion of the Book's message.

Contemporary radical Muslims claim to find in the Qur'an also norms and penalties against blasphemy and apostasy, but in this case too the Qur'an gives no basis to extremist solutions. The death penalty for blasphemy and apostasy, prescribed by some alleged "Islamic states" today, is not Qur'anic but sanctioned by the successive jurisprudence. Practically, the Qur'an does not dealt with blasphemy in the modern sense of the word; in regards to apostasy, for example in 2.217, the judgment is only of God and postponed after the death of the sinner in the afterlife.

Rather, important are the admonitions of "not transgress[ing] the bounds established by God (*hudud Allah*)". In the second sura (The Cow), this is repeated twice: 2.187 and 2.229. Not transgressing the bounds of God (*hudud Allah*) has an orthopractical value and is connected to the previously quoted command of "recommending what is right and forbidding what is wrong". However, although *hudud Allah* like adultery are clearly sanctioned (cfr. 24. 2–4), others, like the consumption of alcoholic beverages, are not. The verse 5.90–91 condemns clearly drinking of wine, but says nothing about the punishment.

THE WAR AND THE *JIHAD*

Fighting is permitted: "Fight in the way of God those who fight you, but do not exceed [the limits] since God does not approve of those who exceed [the limits] [it could be also translated "but do not attack them first because God does not like those who attack"]. Kill them wherever you find them, and turn them out from wherever they turned you out. . . . But if they stop [fighting] God is forgiving and merciful. Fight them until there is no more dissension and religion is restored in God, but if they cease [the struggle] let there be no hostility towards them except for the evildoers" (2.190–193). "Those believers who sit [at home] and are not harmed are not equal to those who struggle for God with their goods and life" (4.95; 8.38–39). As we have seen, the notion of limits is important, since God does not like those who go too far or those who aggress without reason. There cannot be or at least should not be "any compulsion (*ikrah*) in religion" (2.256), a verse that the Muslim reformers and modernists cite enthusiastically to demonstrate that religious tolerance is one of the fundamental values of Islam. Article 10 of the Universal Declaration of Human Rights in Islam refers to 2.256 to permit liberty of worship of religious minorities. Tolerance is valid not only in confrontation with "evildoers" but also for Muslims who abandon their faith and choose other religions. The leading shaykh of Azhar, the famous Islamic university in Cairo, in the time of Nasser, Mahmud Shaltut, argued that the non-compulsion of religion related also to apostates who, despite what the law said, should not then be persecuted or even punished with death. After all, the Qur'an did not provide such a penalty. Believers in any case "fight" not only with their bodies but also through doing good works (5.48), and for this to be possible it is necessary to have peace and relaxed living arrangements "since the believers are brothers to each other, so make peace between brothers and fear God" (49.10).

Certainly, when it speaks of "believers", the Qur'an means Muslims. But this does not mean simply that non-Muslims are "infidels" (*kafirun*). Frequently the terms "infidel" and "evildoer" are linked, and the Qur'an alludes to Meccan polytheists who are enemies of Islam and Muhammad. On religions of the Book, Judaism and Christianity, the Qur'anic position is quite subtle. There are some verses that are decidedly ecumenical, like 5.69 (which is repeated almost identically in 2.62): "For them who believe, there are Jews, Sabians or Christians, those who believe in God and in the last day and do good, they should feel no fear nor distress". There are other verses that are less ecumenical. The language used to describe the Jews, for example, is often hostile, evidently in response to the hostility that they showed to the new religion and its Prophet. Among other things, the Jews are accused of making fun of the Prophet and distorting Scripture (2.104; 4.46), and also of breaking the covenant with God (5.12–13). The language about Christians is milder. We find for example at 5.82–83: "You will find the strongest enemies of those who believe are the Jews and the polytheists, and you will find nearest in their affection to those who believe are those who say 'We are Christians', for among them are priests and monks and those who are not arrogant. And when they come to listen to what was revealed to the Messenger, you will see their eyes filled with tears, since they know what is true. And they say 'We believe! Write us down as witnesses [of the faith]' ". In any case, the Muslims are counseled to keep their distance from the people of the Book: "O you who believe, do not take Jews and Christians as friends. They are only friends to each other, and those among you who seek them as friends will [become] one of them. God really does not guide those who go awry" (5.51).

It is often claimed that the notion of "holy war" is sanctioned by the Qur'an, and the term is equivalent to *jihad*. The term appears in this precise form only four times in the Qur'an. We will quote them all in order to show that it is not possible to say unequivocally that it is the same as the term "holy war". The first is 22.78: "Struggle (*jahidu*) for God in an authentic struggle (*jihad*). He has chosen you and has not given you any difficulties in religion, the religion of our father Abraham". A second passage at 9.24 goes: "If your fathers and your sons, your brothers and your wives and your tribes and the wealth that you have acquired and a business that you worry will start to suffer, and the houses that you like, if these are dearer to you than God and his Messenger and the struggle (*jihad*) in the way of God, then wait until God brings into effect his ruling". In both cases the point could quite easily be to talk about a type of spiritual struggle and not fighting in the military sense. A translation of "holy war" for *jihad* is even less plausible in 25.52: "But do not listen to the unbelievers, but fight them with 'it' in a big struggle (*jihad*)". Bausani means by "it" (*bihi*) the "Word". Abdel Haleem means plainly "the Qur'an", but perhaps it means the "Warner" as al-Zamakhshari in his *Kashshaf*, the huge Mu'tazilite commentary on the Qur'an, has it. The two Jalals, in their *tafsir* or commentary on the Qur'an, which tends to take a more popular line, come down in agreement with Bonelli, and so identify it with the Qur'an. The salafi contemporary Algerian theologian Ibn Badis (he will appear again in Chapter 5 in this volume) has argued that the *jihad* that is linked with fighting through the Qur'an is a *jihad* of propaganda, of persuasion, of preaching. A reference that perhaps comes closer to armed conflict, but really is not that clear on this either, comes in part of 60.1: "If you have come out on a *jihad* on my Way and through the desire to satisfy me, but secretly have affection for them [the enemies], I know well what you hide and what you reveal".

To conclude, the versions of *jihad* that link it with "holy war" are, in each case, not limited to that use, and generally *jihad* is really better translated as a "force" or "engagement", military certainly, but also moral in the path of God. The great theologian al-Ghazali presented one of the clearest arguments for the existence of two meanings of *jihad*. The "great" *jihad* is the struggle for self-purification, in order to conquer the evil inclinations of character and behavior, while the "small" *jihad* corresponds to war. The value of the little *jihad* is inferior, in God's eyes, to the great *jihad*, and many modernists such as Muhammad 'Abduh (we will mention him again in Chapter 5 in this volume as the author of a fundamental Qur'anic commentary) clearly prefer the more defensive sense of *jihad*. In many verses in which combat is mentioned in the Qur'an, the trilateral root *jhd* is not used, but instead the term *qatala* is, which really does mean war. We can look for example at the already quoted verses 2.190–193 that begin with this exhortation: "Fight in the way of God (*qatilu fi sabil Allah*) those who fight you". It is true on the other hand that sometimes (for example, 4.95) the *mujahiduna*, those who conduct the *jihad*, are those who "fight" militarily in the way of God.

LAW AND JURIDICAL PRESCRIPTIONS

Human life is regulated legally: without the government of Laws, society would fall to pieces. As has often been mentioned, especially among Muslims, the Qur'an has normative features and is not only a religious book but also a system of rules. Naturally, if we have to recall that Islam is a religion and a state and that the Qur'an is the "constitution" of the Community, as Sayyid Qutb for one points out, we have to accept that it contains precise legislative rules, both civil and penal, with the corresponding sanctions. We could say, however, like all the Muslim modernists from ʿAbduh to ʿAbd al-Raziq to al-ʿAshmawi, that the Qur'an is principally a religious book and a divine revelation, minimizing its legal content and emphasizing quite accurately that the normative verses in the Book are proportionately very small. If taken together these positions have a fundamental and legitimate conclusion. From this point of view the Qur'an is much more like the Hebrew Bible than the Christian Gospels. The Qur'an like the Bible and unlike the Gospels contains legal prescriptions, some of which are quite minute. However, given also the dimensions of the book, these prescriptions are certainly not more numerous or significant than those that appear in biblical books such as Leviticus or Numbers.

The tendency in contemporary times by some states such as Nigeria, the Sudan, Saudi Arabia or Iran to apply literally Qur'anic penalties in the light of the fact that the Qur'an constitutes one of the sources (together with the *hadith*) of *shariʿa*, religious Law, constitutes without doubt an interpretive challenge. How can we link this approach with the cultural needs of the modern world? In contemporary society a good deal of importance is given to human rights, and that makes it difficult to accept cutting off the hands of thieves or the severe flogging (flogging, not stoning—that is not a Qur'anic sanction) for adulterers. It is sometimes said in support of harsh sanctions that the severity of the Qur'anic penalties was indispensable for regulating a society like that of the anarchic Bedouins at the time of the Prophet. In this regard, the laws of the Talion (an eye for an eye) were certainly present in the Hebrew Bible and no doubt effective where society, as in ancient Israel or former Arabia, lacks a legal system like that of Rome as well as legitimate police forces. This does not deny the fact that Qur'anic penalties, the *hudud*, may challenge human rights. The fact is that, if the Qur'an comes to be identified with the literal world of God, it is possible to interpret it in a rigid way with an obligatory prescriptive content from the penal point of view. However, it could be suggested, as the Sudanese Mahmud Taha (coming up again in Chapter 4 in this volume) did, that we should contextualize historically the Medinan revelations. The issue is still open in Islamic thought. It really is an issue of what we take to be the main verses that outline explicitly the legal norms.

The verse 4.3 sanctions the acceptability of polygamy. I say sanction because although it is possible to have four wives, the text states that if there is the possibility of being unjust to one of the wives, it is better to marry only one. Many modernists like 'Abduh and Abu Zayd have suggested that it is impossible to be just with four wives, and so the Qur'an in effect recommends monogamy. As in all patriarchal societies, the Qur'an affirms clearly the superiority of man over women and of the husband over the wife. However, it does not prescribe the segregation of women (apart from the specifically mentioned wives of Muhammad), nor does it oblige the use of the veil or the burqa and anything else like that. There are references to shame and modesty, for example in 24.31: "Say to all the believers that they should lower their gaze and guard their modesty and not display their beauty, except what appears externally, and they should cover up their breasts and not show their beauty to anyone except their husbands". Modesty is also a masculine virtue, and it is declared to be entirely appropriate for men too. Verses 4.7–14 contain precise rules on how to pass on property, and there are other passages that touch on this topic. They deal with very dry and minute details, and they constitute the basis to family law, at least in so far as the leaving of bequests is concerned. The verse 2.226 and what follows deal with divorce and rejection, and we come to see how to regulate a legal situation that was, in the Arabia of Muhammad's time, extremely chaotic and difficult, and that ameliorated to a degree the situation of women in contemporary Arabia, recognizing their personal legal rights and their right to dispose of their property as they wished. Contemporary modernists have emphasized that the Qur'an (and Islam) was the first to recognize the existence of a judicial identity for all women, and yet the literal interpretation of the text has interfered with what would otherwise be a positive teaching. The seventh century was not an adequate arena for determining rights in modern society. But the modernists and the contemporary apologists generally point to the positive nature of the principle. Verses 24.2–6 discipline adultery (punished by flogging, and the testimony of four eyewitnesses is necessary before someone who is accused can be punished). Verse 5.38 establishes the penalty for theft (cutting off the hand), and 2.178–179 for murder (death). There are also food restrictions like the previously quoted 5.90 that forbids the consumption of wine or 5.3 that forbids the consumption of carrion, blood, pork and other things also. Food taboos are widespread in different cultures and societies, and the Hebrew Bible has a lot more of them than the Qur'an. The rules about the division of booty (especially 8.41) naturally have a meaning in a Bedouin society where raids are important, but today are less significant. A verse that remains highly relevant is 2.275, which talks about the total and definitive illegitimacy of usury. It is important because it has conditioned, and still conditions, the development of an Islamic banking system. Many artifices are used in order to preserve the principle of profit while maintaining a prohibition on interest.

Although a certain severity in the sacred text emerges, the Muslim Community sees itself as following the "middle way", referring here to the famous verse 2.143: "We have made you a Community in the middle (*wasatan*)". Naturally, as we have seen, the Qur'an organized Medinan society in a way specified by the Prophet. The fact is indisputable that the fundamental ethical principle of human social life is solidarity. Solidarity was a fundamental condition of tribal life and of the clan. But Muhammad, inspired by God, took an existing community and turned it into a community of believers. We have already noted the verse that urges all believers to be siblings of each other. But the passage that is perhaps even more significant is the so-called verse "of Piety" (*ayat al-birr*), 2.177, whose tone is clearly evangelical: "True piety does not consist in turning the face to the East or the West, but true piety is believing in God and in the Last Day, in the angels and in the Book and in the Prophets and to spend your money out of love of God for your relatives, for orphans, the poor, the travellers, and to those who ask [for alms] or to rescue [prisoners], to complete your prayers, pay the tithe, to be faithful to the contracts that you have made, and to be patient in the face of all tribulations and adversities, and when [there is] distress".

PROPHECY

The mediation between God and humanity is guaranteed by prophecy. We have already seen that Islam is a prophetic religion. It is certainly worth stressing that the Qur'an itself is replete with stories of prophecy. Islam recognizes, as a matter of rule, two kinds of prophet: the "legislative" prophet and the "warning" prophet. The "legislative" prophet is really the "Messenger" or "Envoy" or "Apostle" as the word was unfortunately translated some decades ago: the Arabic term is *rasul*. In the history of prophecy there are said to be six main legislative prophets, messengers who heard directly from God, who we have already listed in Chapter 1 in this volume: Adam, Noah, Abraham, Moses, Jesus and Muhammad, which represents the line of prophecy. Each of them brought a book. The prophets who mainly warn are said, according to tradition, to number 124,000. Each people has had its prophet, someone who speaks the language of the people. The more general Arabic world for prophet is *nabi*, a term that is used in the Qur'an particularly for the biblical prophets.

The Qur'an traces minutely—although not systematically and with evident narrative links with the Hebrew Bible—the notion of prophecy that we have just outlined. We should note some essential references. The Islamic revelation is acknowledged as being in the Abrahamic tradition: "[God] revealed to you [Muhammad] the Book according to the Truth, confirming what preceded it, and he revealed earlier the Torah and the Gospels as a guide for humanity" (3.3). The true faith is really one, neither Judaism nor Christianity, but Islam as the pristine monotheism: "the religion (*milla*) of our father Abraham, it was he who named you Muslims from the beginning" (22.78). We have already seen how the Qur'an alludes to Islam as a natural religion (30.30) and "definitive" (5.3). Abraham was the father of monotheism, but he was neither a Jew nor a Christian, but *hanif*, a pure monotheist, someone in love with the Unity of God and opposed to polytheism (3.67; 6.79; and 6.161). Each community has been sent a divine messenger (many verses, through to 10.47), even directed to animals, and every type of creature has its appropriate prophet. There are many references to "Arab" prophets quoted in the Qur'an, prophets sent particularly to the tribes on the Arabian peninsula, like Hud, Salih and Shu'ayb. The stories of biblical prophets stretch from Noah (to whom is dedicated sura 71) to Jonah (sura 10 [Yunus]) and from David to Solomon (who Islam considers prophets), but especially Moses, whose story is narrated in detail (although not always clearly), and we will not give quotes here since they are scattered around the text. The fundamental elements are described similarly in both: birth and his first years, the face-to-face meeting with God near the burning bush, the mission in Egypt and the confrontation with Pharaoh, the receiving of the slabs of the Law on Sinai, the gold calf. W. M. Watt and R. Bell (1970) have often argued that the Mosaic story in the Qur'an is incoherent and that if someone did not know first the Biblical story it would be difficult to understand it. However, this criticism is only partially valid. It is true that an understanding of the biblical account helps in understanding the Qur'anic account. But it is not a matter of incoherence so much as a reflection in the holy Book of Islam of a tradition that probably is not entirely consonant with biblical "orthodoxy" and in which some particulars are narrated differently. It is certainly possible that Muhammad's audience would have known in quite a detailed way the story that he narrated.

Quite similar to the biblical story also is the account given of Joseph, the "most beautiful story ever told", to which is dedicated an entire sura, sura 12. The hostility of the brothers at Joseph's relationship with Jacob, the journey to Egypt, the story of the wife of Potiphar who fell in love with him and tempted him, the interpretation of the dreams, the elevation by Pharaoh, the meeting again with Jacob—all these important elements of the story are found in the Qur'an. However, they have a different meaning, more on the level of the details than on the general narration of the story. For example, while the Bible suggests that the betrayal of Joseph was the result of a sudden decision, the Qur'an seems to emphasize its premeditation. Also, when the Bible attributes, among other things, the hatred of the brothers for Joseph that led him to speak badly of them to Jacob, the Qur'an has nothing of this and makes him the innocent victim of the evildoing of his brothers. It is possible that the biblical stories that circulated in Mecca and Medina at the time of the Prophet contained different versions of what came to be fixed in the canonical tradition.

There are three miraculous stories in sura 18, "The Cave". The first is the legend of the "seven sleepers of Ephesus", a legend of Christian origin that, sanctified by Qur'anic authority, has become very much part of Islamic tradition. God kept alive for three centuries, miraculously asleep, seven Christians from Ephesus to save them from persecution by the emperor Decius. Next there is a curious story that involves Moses (probably not linked with the biblical character) and a mysterious person, the "Green One" (al-Khidr). They travelled together, and Moses saw his companion doing some remarkable things but without really understanding why. Finally, there is the legend "Of the Two Horned One", which tradition identifies with Alexander the Great. This is a remnant of the romance of Alexander that was spread around the Near and Middle East in popular culture. The Two Horned One fights and controls the savage populations of Gog and Magog. The chapter finishes with an invitation to respect the monotheistic religion. But the exaltation of Unity and the omnipotence of God are not the only themes of sura 18, for here the Qur'an also discusses the justice of God, the theodicy that is incomprehensible to human reason. God is sovereign and just, and that means that he is justified in doing what seems unjustifiable to humans. However, God has fixed the Laws, and in the system of Laws theodicy is resolved. This could be the theological significance of the story of Moses and al-Khidr, and others have also noted the eschatological message of the sura.

Naturally, the Qur'an contains an account of Christianity. Christ is the Word of God, but not his son nor part of the Trinity—the most relevant verse is 4.171: "O people of the Book, do not put anything excessive in your religion (*din*) and do not say of God anything except the truth. In fact, the Messiah 'Isa (Jesus) son of Mary, is a Messenger of God, his Word that He put in Mary, a Spirit coming from him. Believe in God and in his Messengers and do not say 'Three'. Stop it! It will be better for you! God is One God, praise be to Him, and does not have sons!"

It is clear that the Qur'an does not consider Trinitarian doctrine as "monotheism", although some verses seem to understand Trinity as tritheism—for example 5.72–73: "They are unbelievers who say that 'God is the Messiah, son of Mary'. . . . They are unbelievers who say that God is the third of three (*thalith thalatha*)'. . .".

However, 4.171 is, like sura 112, a complex verse. It defines Jesus as (a) Messiah (*masih*); (b) messenger (*rasul*); (c) word (*kalima*); and (d) spirit (*ruh*). Muhammad is not defined in a such rich manner in one time. Let us briefly consider the four attributes.

First of all, Jesus is not a Messiah in the biblical or Christian sense: his duty is not to be a redeemer and a savior, although in Islam he will have a decisive eschatological role at the end of the times. Jesus—as we have already said—is one of the great six legislator prophets (*rasul*). More problematic is the attribute of *kalima*, "word". Understanding *kalima* in the Christian sense of *Logos* is undoubtedly a strain both linguistically and theologically. Likely, the Qur'an means that Jesus has been a "tongue" through which God transmitted His "word". In Islamic tradition, rather, are Muhammad as "perfect man" and the same Qur'an to be the *Logos*. Finally, Jesus is "spirit". The concept of spirit in the Qur'an is highly controversial (O'Shaughnessy 1953) and can allude to the Angel of revelation, to the divine order (*amr*) structuring the universe, to the inspiration God "breathes" into the prophets, and so on. Possibly, Jesus is spirit insofar as he is a mean of communication between God and humankind.

Jesus is said to have been conceived miraculously by Mary the Virgin, apart from the hints in 4.171, while 19.16–34 tells of the appearance of an angel to Mary and the immaculate conception in a very similar manner to the Gospel story (notwithstanding some very different details), and when the baby is born he has miraculous properties, which is only also recorded in the New Testament Apocrypha. Islam fosters a profound veneration for Mary. The Christians have not acknowledged this and have concentrated negatively on those aspects of the Qur'anic account that contradict the official Christian tradition. This does not apply just to Mary. For example, according to the Qur'an, Jesus was not crucified but was raised up from the cross by a double (4.157–158). This reflects a divergent doctrine of heretical Christians like the Docetists. It is certainly the case that the death of Jesus on the cross is fundamental for Christian dogma for the purposes of redemption. But Islam does not share the idea of original sin, and salvation is a direct affair between the believer and God. Adam and Eve sinned certainly in Eden, but their fault is not transferable to successive human generations as Christianity suggests. The polemic against the Trinity is brought up in other places, and it is said that the adoration given to a God who is three is blasphemy (see 5.111, where it says that the Trinity is composed of God, Jesus and Mary). In other places the polemic continues against the idea that Christ is the "physical" son of God (5.110; 9.30). It is certainly possible to argue that the Muslims do not interpret the Trinity correctly, transforming it into belief in three gods. But the idea of God who is both one and three is not immediately graspable from a rational point of view. For its part the Qur'an contains a firm condemnation throughout of all attempts at fragmenting the essence of the One God in whatever variety of ways this might be attempted. Analogously, Islam refutes central aspects of Christian dogma like the sacraments. It is hostile in particular to the idea of communion (the philosopher Averroes ironically and cynically wonders if the Christians are set upon "eating their Lord"). We may certainly have the impression that Muslims do not always appreciate the spiritual essence of sacramental issues, but, as Bausani notes, in Islam "the sacrament is blasphemy and magic, in so far as in a way it constrains God, *ex opere operato* [to act beyond His willing because of external factors] and through human hands, to determine operations. Dogma and sacraments, like humanist and magic elements, that explain or address the production of necessary laws in the area of the divine, are not understandable in relation to the God of Islam who is entirely free, personal and unconstrained" (Bausani 1980: 42–43). This shows how far Qur'anic Christology is from the Christian vision and constitutes without doubt a potential obstacle for theological dialogue. With Muhammad and the Qur'an, in the end religion is perfected and prophecy is sealed. The prophetic chain is definitively concluded. Muhammad is only a man (18.110 and in many other verses also), but he is given the role of the seal of the prophets (33.40).

The Qur'an contains various accounts of the prophetic experience of Muhammad, and they not only reveal the humanity and the frailty but constitute an implicit conferment of honesty on his inspiration. Covered in a cloak (73.1 and 74.1) in order to resist the effect of cold and fear that occurred during the granting of revelation, he had direct visionary experience: "Your companion is not deceived or mistaken and does not talk of any passion. This is nothing other than the revelation that is revealed, that he was told by a mighty Power, weighed down with understanding. For he spoke and came closer and was two bow lengths away or perhaps even less, and revealed to his servant what he revealed, nor did [the eyes] of his heart deny what he saw [physically]" (53.2–11). The Prophet "suffers" the revelation and comes to warn to not hurry because God knows better the times in which it is right to talk to Him to be in line for explanation (75.16–19). Muhammad is sometimes reported for a sin of pride. When he was talking with some wealthy Meccans, he was disturbed by a poor person who asked for his advice. "He frowned and turned away" because he was angry, but God reprimanded him severely": "As for him who is rich, you are concerned with him although it does not concern you if he is not purified. But for him who came to you worried and frightened [of God] you paid no attention" (80.5–10). Finally, we should discuss the "Satanic verses". In sura 53.19–20 we read: "What do you think of Allat, 'Uzza and Manat, the three idols?" These three goddesses are the most venerated in pre-Islamic Arabia. Well, according to some traditions, that are accepted quite frankly by "orthodoxy", originally these verses were followed by another two that say: "They are sublime goddesses and their intercession is foreseeably certain". Muhammad is said here to have concealed a compromise with the Meccan oligarchy (defending the possibility of an infraction of monotheism). But such words were an inspiration not from God but from Satan and were soon abrogated (apparently the next day), so the two "Satanic verses" disappeared from the Qur'an. This is a further confirmation of the honesty of Muhammad and demonstrates how the conquest of the true faith found in its Prophet an appropriate and rigorous champion.

SUMMARY

In this chapter we have dealt with

- The issue of the alleged inconsistency of the Qur'anic text and the new theories about its coherence.
- The concept of God in the Qur'an, emphasizing the characteristics of His essence (monotheism) and His creative power.
- The beautiful names of God.
- The mystical and metaphysical verses, like the Light verse.
- The concept of the human being in the Qur'an and the problem of free will.
- The political and juridical contents of the Holy Book, studying the concept of *jihad*, and the penalties prescribed by the Holy text.
- The verses regarding the people of the Book, and the prophetic tradition in the Qur'an, from the Biblical to the Arab prophets to Muhammad.
- The Qur'anic Christology.

REFERENCES/READINGS

Avicenna, *Livre des Directives et des Remarques*, edited by A.M. Goichon, Vrin, Paris 1951.

Bausani, A. *L'Islam*, Garzanti, Milano 1980.

Campanini, M. *La Sura della Caverna: Meditazione filosofica sull'Unicità di Dio*, La Nuova Italia, Firenze 1986.

Cook, M. *Commanding Right and Forbidding Wrong in Islamic Thought*, Cambridge University Press, Cambridge 2000a.

Cook, M. *The Koran: A Very Short Introduction*, Oxford University Press, Oxford-New York 2000b.

Cuypers, M. *Le Festin. Lecture de la sourate al-Ma'ida*, Lethellieux, Paris 2007.

Dall'Oglio, P. *Speranza nell'Islam. Interpretazione della prospettiva escatologica di Corano 18*, Marietti, Genova 1991.

al-Farabi, *On the Perfect State*, edited by R. Walzer, Clarendon Press, Oxford 1985 (Italian translation by M. Campanini, *La Città virtuosa*, Rizzoli, Milano 1996).

Farrin, R. *Structure and Qur'anic Interpretation: A Study of Symmetry and Coherence in Islam's Holy Text*, White Cloud Press, Ashland, OR 2014.

Gabrieli, F. *Storia della letteratura araba*, Sansoni-Accademia, Florence-Milan 1967.

al-Ghazali, *Kitab al-arba'in fi usul al-din (The Forty Principles of Religion)*, Maktabat al-Jindi, Cairo 1970.

al-Ghazali, *The Pearls of the Koran*, trans. M. Abul Quasem, Kegan Paul, London 1983 (Italian translation by M. Campanini, *Le Perle del Corano*, Rizzoli, Milano 2000).

al-Ghazali, *Mishkat al-anwar*, Alam al-Kutub, Beirut 1986 (English translation *The Niche of Lights*, ed. D. Buchman, Brigham Young University Press, Provo 1998).

Al-Ghazali, *Maqsad al-asnà fi Sharh ma'ani asma Allah al-husnà*, Jaffanwa Jabi, Limassol 1987 (English translation by al-Ghazali, *The Ninety-nine Beautiful Names of God*, trans. D. Burrell and N. Daher, The Islamic Texts Society, Cambridge 1995).

Laoust, H. *Le Traité de Droit Publique d'Ibn Taymiyyah*, Institut Français d'Archèologie Orientale, Damascus 1939.

Merad, A. *Ibn Badis Commentateur du Coran*, Geuthner, Paris 1971.

Mir, M. *Coherence in the Qur'an: A Study of al-Islahi's Concept of Nazm*, American Trust Publications, Indianapolis 1986.

Nicholson, R. *Studies in Islamic Mysticism*, Idarah-iAdabiyat-iDelli, Delhi 1981.

O'Shaughnessy, T. *The Development of the Meaning of Spirit in the Qur'an*, Orientalia Christiana Analecta, Roma 1953.

Parrinder, G. *Jesus in the Qur'an*, Faber, London 1965.

Robinson, N. *Christ in Islam and Christianity: The Representation of Jesus in the Qur'an and the Classical Muslim Commentaries*, Macmillan, Basingstoke 1991.

Tottoli, R. *I profeti biblici nella tradizione islamica*, Paideia, Brescia 1999 (English translation *Biblical Prophets in the Qur' an and Muslim Literature*, Curzon, Richmond 2002).

Walker, P. *Early Philosophical Shiism: The Ismaili Neoplatonism of Abu Ya'qub al-Sijistani*, Cambridge University Press, Cambridge 1993.

4

THE QUR'AN AND THE QUR'ANIC SCIENCES

HOW THE QUR'AN DEFINES ITSELF

The Qur'an is the Word of God. A view accepted widely among both Muslims and orientalists is that the Qur'an has the same function in Islam as Christ in Christianity. Christ is the incarnation of God on earth; the Qur'an is the Book in which the Word, the Word of God in fact, is so to speak "made flesh" in the midst of all human beings. We have already seen how the earlier theologians argued over whether the Qur'an was created or uncreated and have largely accepted that it is possible to say that the Qur'an can be seen to accord with the Ash'arite position rather than the Mu'tazilite. We read on this: "it is a glorious Qur'an [inscribed] on a 'Preserved Tablet' (*lawh mahfuz*)" (85.21–22). In other places there is talk of a celestial archetype or "Mother of the Book" (*umm al-kitab*), a sort of matrix from which the Qur'an was produced "physically" as men wrote it down, read and recited it (3.7; 13.39). Of course, all these passages do not prove univocally that the Qur'an was not uncreated, but the letter of the text seems to point rather to support of the Ash'arite position. The Qur'an, whether or not it is uncreated, is revealed in a human language, "in a clear Arabic" (see 26.195), a holy language, but it is "a message for everyone" (38.87), "a warning for all creatures" (6.90). Whatever we have seen about the revelation being in Arabic, it is a universal message sent down for all people.

The question of the *Arabicity* of the Qur'an has been connected with its *inimitability*. It would be useful to return to this issue because it may help us to understand more clearly the value that the Book has for Muslims. The famous medieval commentator al-Baydawi summarizes a passage of sura Joseph (12.1–3; the translation is by Helmut Gätje):

Alif, Lam, Ra. These are the signs of the clear Book. We have sent it down as an Arabic Qur'an; perhaps you will understand [. . .].

These are the signs (or "verses", *ayat*) of the clear Book: (the word) "these" (*tilka*) is a demonstrative pronoun referring to the (following) verses of the sura. By the "Book" here is meant the sura itself. The meaning is (therefore): these verses constitute the verses of the sura which presents itself clearly as inimitability (*i'jaz*); or, as that of which the meanings are clear; or, as that which makes clear (*bayan*) to anyone who reflects upon it, that it comes from God; or, that which makes clear to the Jews what they have asked about. [. . .]

As an Arabic Qur'ân: this part (of the whole revelation) is designated here as Qur'an. In origin this word is a generic noun which is applicable to the whole (of the class) as well as to a part of it. It then became predominant as a proper name referring to the whole. [. . .]

Perhaps you will understand: this is the reason why God sent down the Book in this (Arabic) form. The meaning is (therefore): We have sent it down to you as something that is composed in your own language or can be recited in your own language, so that you will be able to understand it and grasp its meanings; or, that you will employ your intellect and (through it) discover that the account, out of the mouth of a man like this [Muhammad] who could not produce a (comparable) account (previously), is a matchless miracle (*mu'jiz*) which one can conceive only as having been revealed (*sic*).

(Gätje 1976: 52f.)

As can be seen from this passage, the Qur'an has many names that it itself acknowledges. The Qur'an defines itself in many passages, but it is also clearly the "Book" (*Kitab*), a term that is perhaps better translated as "Scripture" as argued by Daniel Madigan. There are other expressions that refer to it, in relation especially to its function, or sometimes to its content. One of the terms is *aya* (plural *ayat*), or "sign", a term that as we have seen can mean also "verse" in the sense that a "sign" of God can be represented in a Book. *Ayat*, according to Watt and Bell (1970), can indicate the following: the natural phenomena that are the signs of divine power and providence; the events or daily partners in a prophetic mission; the performed signs of a messenger/prophet; the signs that are delivered by the Qur'an. In all these cases the Qur'an presents itself as an invitation, a suggestion to listen to God and the Prophet, to reflect on reality and to think of God and upon God.

Often the term Qur'an in the sacred text seems to mean recitation. Qur'an is derived from the verb *qara'a* that, significantly, is the verb with which the first sura opens. The angel Gabriel appears to Muhammad and orders him: "*Iqra*". There are a variety of semantic renderings that can translate it as "Read!" (the Book), but that could be a problem given that the "orthodox" Islamic view is that the Prophet was illiterate. Bausani translates it as "Shout!", but a probably more accurate translation would be "Recite!", as translated by Arberry (Abdel Haleem has "Read!"). The Qur'an is really a Book that is recited and needs to be recited (see for example 16.98). It was transmitted directly by God (see especially 4.82), who "sent it down" "as an Arabic Qur'an, so that you might understand it" (12.2). The Qur'an is "the" revelation, but "this particular" Qur'an (see for instance 6.19) is what was directly revealed to Muhammad. However, "this Qur'an" is the book in which God has explained to all humans every kind of similitude (17.89). Watt and Bell (1970) have suggested that the Book (here equivalent to Scripture) defines itself as Qur'an especially in the first phases of revelation while in the later period the term *Kitab* was more used where this is equivalent to "Book or "Scripture". The thesis is not that convincing, and, in the Medinan suras, 2.185 for instance, Qur'an is used just as much as in the Meccan suras, about six out of twelve times, as compared with *Kitab*. In any case, *Kitab* is repeated so many times that it should be regarded as having several meanings. In 29.51, the *Kitab* is revealed directly to Muhammad and so to his community, but, in other contexts, as in 2.2 or in 32.2, it is evidently a universal revelation, provided for all people, in which there is no "doubt" (*rayb*). *Qur'an* and *Kitab* are then terms that have a range of functions.

Another way in which the Qur'an defines itself is as *bayan*, which means "explication" or "proof" or better clear demonstration and evidence of the intentions of God. The word appears twice in the Qur'an, first in 3.138: "This is a proof for men and a guide and a warning for those who fear God". It appears a second time in 55.4, although in this case to translate (with Bausani) *bayan* as "clear expression" might be unsatisfactory, while a more correct translation would go: "[God] has created man and has taught him the clear proof [the Qur'an]" (Arberry translates it as "explanation", and Abdel Haleem as "clear lesson"). Another name for the Qur'an is *Furqan*, derived from the verbal root *frq*: this means "discrimination". The Qur'an discriminates between the true and the false, between the permitted and the illegitimate, between before and after. The Furqan is said to have been given to Moses together with the Kitab (2.53). It is linked with the Torah and the Gospels (3.3). In 8.41, alluding to the battle of Badr in which the Muslims defeated the Meccans for the first time, the Qur'an says: "what we revealed to Our servant [Muhammad] on the day of furqan" because (perhaps) it was the day on which it was settled and decided where the truth lay (on the side of the Muslims who defeated the unbelievers in the battle). As we have seen, the terms have a precise meaning in a precise context.

TAFSIR: THE TRADITIONAL COMMENTARY

The many names of the Qur'an show how it is possible to approach it in a variety of ways, as a text that discloses the signs of God, as a text that outlines the evident proofs of the truth of prophecy and revelation and as a text that distinguishes the range of values, assesses them and imposes them on human behavior. This leads us obviously to the problem of interpretation. In Arabic there are two terms that refer to the interpretive activity, *tafsir* and *ta'wil*. The difference between them and their applications has been recently summarized by Poonawala: "According to the opinions of most scholars, *ta'wil* is based on reason and personal opinion (*ra'y*), while *tafsir* is based on the material transmission of the Prophet himself or through his companions or his successors in the form of hadith (*athar*). On this view *ta'wil* is generally defined as 'interpretation according to rationality' while *tafsir* is 'interpretation in accord with what has been transmitted'. So *tafsir* concerns roughly transmission of stories (*riwaya*) while *ta'wil* is roughly about 'knowing the sophisticated or complex meaning (*diraya*)'".

Tafsir appears to be traditional commentary, highly linguistic and narrative, putting a lot of emphasis on the stories of the prophets, the episodes of revelation, and grammatical studies. By contrast, *ta'wil* takes a more speculative line and is more appropriately defined as "hermeneutical". It is worth noting that the term *ta'wil* comes from the verb *awwala* that in its primary meaning refers to "returning to the sources", to the origins. Both words are used in the Qur'an. *Tafsir* has a sole use in 25.33: "And no issue is put to you [Muhammad] without Us [God] revealing to you the true [meaning] (*haqq*) and the better interpretation (*tafsir*)". *Ta'wil* by contrast appears about seventeen times, especially with the meaning of interpreting dreams, but in some verses it takes on a rich meaning going in the direction of a hermeneutics in the philosophical sense of the term.

When we discuss *tafsir*, a fundamental distinction can be made about the concept of commentary according to ordinary authority stemming from the prophetic traditions (*tafsir bi'l-ma'thur*) and commentary according to the use of the intellect (*tafsir bi'l-ra'y*). This second type of commentary comes close to the hermeneutics of *ta'wil* but is not exactly the same. In the first type of commentary, the interpretive method follows the procedures of the traditional Islamic sciences, especially the science of hadith, the deeds and sayings of the Prophet Muhammad. The clash between the two kinds of commentary reflects naturally a dialectic that is always very much there in the Islamic intellectual world and has profound repercussions in modernity: the dialectic between reverence for the text and tradition as opposed to the desire for a progressive and rationalist reading of the revealed passage (this topic will be raised again in the next chapter when we look at interpretation in contemporary times). Now, in commentary according to authority and tradition, great importance is given to the sciences that deal with literal meaning and legal exegesis, the literal and legal being linked in the text through the connection between the linguistic expression and its historical context. Among these sciences in first place is grammar, together with lexicography and orthography, indispensable to the study of the language in which the holy text has been revealed. In the second place there are the "stories of the prophets", the pious reconstruction of the accounts of the great patriarchs who appear in the religious stories in the Qur'an. A contribution absolutely central to the comprehension of the Qur'an involves the traditions (*hadith*) of the Prophet Muhammad that explain and reflect the prescriptions of the Book and that have taken on a sacred authority, almost sometimes in the sense of being treated as of equal significance to the revealed text. There are also the "causes" or "occasions" of revelation (*asbab al-nuzul*) that minutely, verse by verse, record the circumstances in which God decided to "bring down" his word. We can see how the historical and legal questions have great relevance in the discipline of commentary according to authority and tradition. This has the effect of reducing the role of theology, since it has an only instrumental function and does not seem to be one of the principal preoccupations of the commentators. In fact, it is not unusual in Islam for the attitude to be taken to the science of God, the "theologia", of limiting it to the study of his acts, while maintaining that the divine essence remains beyond human understanding. It is not important so much what *thing* God is as compared with what he *does* (creates, reveals, judges, punishes, loves and so on). In this sense, the approach to the text by the commentators (*mufassirun*) is not taken up so much with devising in the Qur'an how to go about a rationalist investigation of God that is really not possible, as it is with understanding the actual structure of the text and its implications on the level of its formal constitution. In the next two paragraphs we will look at the sciences of the Qur'an again and that particular area called the "abrogating and the abrogated".

The interpretative activity of the Qur'an started very quickly, and the companion of the Prophet Ibn 'Abbas (d. 688) acquired the status of a highly influential commentator. Ibn 'Abbas and his disciples (the *mufassirun*) were directly part of his school for the whole of the eighth century and worked especially on the ambiguous expressions and grammatical investigations. Exegetes belonging to successive generations, like Ibn Qutayba (d. 889), have sought to clear up the obscure aspects and doubts surrounding the Qur'an using in particular linguistic analyses. We can see this in the very titles of the works of Ibn Qutayba that allude to particular Qur'anic sciences, *Gharib al-Qur'an* (The obscure features of the Qur'an) and *Mushkil al-Qur'an* (Problematic aspects of the Qur'an). A work that must be treated very seriously is that by Muhammad ibn Jarir al-Tabari (d. 923), a Persian scholar who, as well as his monumental commentary, wrote a very valuable *History of Prophets and Kings*, a venerable mine of information especially on the first centuries of Islamic history after the Hijra. Al-Tabari composed a commentary that constitutes one of the better examples of exegesis according to authority and tradition, because of the huge number of *hadith* used in the analysis. To give an idea of this method, it is enough to quote a passage of his commentary (in the translation of Gätje):

> "The vision (*al-absar*) (of men) reaches (*tudrikuhu*) Him not, but He reaches the vision (of men)" (6, 103). Some exegetes maintain that the meaning is as follows: the vision (of men) does not fully grasp (*ahata*) Him, but will be grasped by Him. To be cited (as authorities) for this view are (the following): Yunus Ibn 'Abd Allah Ibn 'Abd al-Hakam has related to us on the basis of (a chain of authorities going back to) Khalid Ibn 'Abd al-Rahman and Abu 'Arfaja the following quotation from 'Atiyya al-'Aufi concerning God's words: "Upon that day (of Resurrection) there will be radiant faces, gazing (*naziratun*) upon their Lord" (sura 75,22): "They shall gaze upon God, yet their vision shall not reach Him because of His greatness, while His vision shall reach them". This is mentioned in God's words: "The vision (of men) reaches Him not, but He reaches the vision (of men)". [. . .] Hannad has related to us on the authority of (a chain of witnesses going back to) Waki', Isma'il Ibn Abi Khalid, 'Amir al-Sha'bi e Masruq, the following words of 'A'isha [the favorite wife of Muhammad]: "If someone reports to you that the Messenger of God has seen his Lord, then he lies". (God's words however read:) "The vision (of men) reaches Him not, but He reaches the vision (of men)".

> (Gätje 1976: 56)

Al-Tabari was hostile to playing around with the obvious meaning of the text, maintaining throughout that the metaphorical or ambiguous verses (*mutashabihat*) are much fewer than is often thought and should be left to the interpretation of God himself (as we shall see later on). He argues that literal interpretation only be abandoned in very serious and extreme cases, for which reason he opposes the rational hermeneutics of the Mu'tazilites. Such a hermeneutics is not followed by an author like al-Zamakhshari (d. 1144), who wrote a large work devoted to philological questions and had a clear Mu'tazilite orientation in theology, accepting the principle of human free will and holding onto various anthropomorphic concepts in the description of God. The commentary of al-Zamakhshari, entitled *al-Kashshaf* or "The Disclosure", is especially significant from the point of view of the method already described where the Qur'anic text can be read in the light of allusions and metaphors.

Other important medieval *tafsir* or commentaries are those by al-Baydawi (d. c. 1286), who does not display particular originality but is held in the Sunni world to be the best, and Fakhr al-Din al-Razi (1149–1209), which, although unfinished, provides evidence of philosophical traces that were customary in the theological thought of the author. He is a characteristic example of a rationalist commentator. The style of one part is very different from another, which is to a degree independent of what precedes it, and rather rationalist in tone. The work of Fakhr al-Din al-Razi has been criticized as not really falling into line with the Islamic point of view and as pushing the limits of exegesis much further than is appropriate. Two later Egyptian polymaths, Jalal al-Din al-Mahalli and Jalal al-Din al-Suyuti (the latter living between 1445 and 1505), have summarized centuries of the science of *tafsir* in a commentary that came to enjoy considerable popular regard. Their work is not original but distills the traditional wisdom of the commentators, adequately emphasizing the concept of the Unity of God.

To give an idea of the work of the Jalalayn, as they came to be called, let us look at their commentary on the very famous Throne verse (2.255, where the Throne is understood to be like the "sciences" of God):

(God! There is no god but He) because He is the only one to be really adored in his existence (but He, the Living) who is permanent in eternity (the self-sufficient) who is at the highest level [of potential and perfection] and confers order and structure on creation (no slumber can affect him) or sluggishness (nor sleep. Everything in the heavens and on earth belongs to Him) the Kingdom (*mulk*), Creation (*khalq*) and adoration ('*ubayd*) (who may) really no one can (intercede with Him except with his permission?) He preserves his exclusivity (He knows what is before them) meaning all people (and what is behind them) evidently the things of this world and of the world to come (while He is not limited in his knowledge) because no-one knows what things He knows (except as He wills) that people know of Him through the medium of the information brought by the prophets (His Throne extends over the heavens and the earth) obviously, his knowledge embraces both. It could also be said, the Throne understands them together thanks to divine majesty. There is a *hadith*—"The seven heavens are on the Throne like seven dirham thrown on a shield" [like seven coins of low value are contained in an important and precious thing] (He is not fatigued) at the weight (of guarding it) meaning the heavens and the earth (and He is the Highest) for everything mentioned here he created in virtue of his power (the Magnificent) the Great.

(Jalalayn n.d.)

Emphasizing the lack of originality in the commentators runs the risk of giving the reader a false impression. Even in works that are little more than compilations of early works or that limit themselves essentially to stylistic and grammatical questions, it is possible to find some exegetical pearls. Let us consider for instance the excursus of al-Baydawi of 2.164: "In the creation of the heavens and the earth, in the difference between night and day, and in the vessels that sail the seas and are so useful to men, in the water that God makes comes down from the sky renewing the earth with life after its death, an earth that He fills with cattle, where he does not alter the winds and the clouds that flow between heaven and earth—[in all these things] are signs for people who are capable of understanding". The commentator points out that the signs quoted in the Book constitute various types of possible existence that can be conceptualized in a variety of ways. Now, as they obey a logic of design, we ought to posit the existence of a wise and powerful creature who acts in accordance with his wisdom and intelligence. That this creature is One is proved by the fact that, if there were two, one would have to be weaker and one stronger than the other, and weakness is not a characteristic of divinity. In conclusion, al-Baydawi utilizes the Qur'anic verse to produce a proof of the existence of God in the style of Ash'arite theology.

Notwithstanding what we have said, commentary according to authority and tradition is more an enquiry into the formal aspects and the historical circumstances of the composition of the text. Apart from some sporadic cases, the theological and theoretical interests are really rather minimal. The commentators are already very much conditioned or committed to accepting the inimitability of the text and the extraordinary respect reserved for that which they believe to be

the authentic and direct word of God. This implies a genuine veneration for the language, structure and evidence of the text. In effect, as
the shrewd contemporary Tunisian thinker H'mida Ennaifer (1998)
has pointed out, in traditional commentary *the meaning of the text is
immutable* in the sense that it is regarded as transcending historicity.
The truth arrives outside of history, external to the world and the
living context of human beings. It is one thing to pay attention to
the reconstruction of the historical origins of the verses and quite
another to consider the possibility that the obvious sense could have
been modified in the course of the centuries by people who changed
it in line with the social reality in which the text came to play a role.
The tendency to exalt the past has been defined as anti-utopianism
and has played a major role in forming the mindset of the intellectuals of classical Islam. While Islamic culture was expanding and
productive (between the ninth and the twelfth centuries especially),
this defect could be hidden, but it really emerged once the conditions developed that produced moments of crisis or decadence. As
Ennaifer (1998) has argued, the tradition of Qur'anic commentary is
designed to be persuasive and apologetic, not constructive, but defensive. This analysis contains a lot of truth, but it is important as always
not to exaggerate or rely on generalizations. The Qur'an has always
had a primary function in the individual life of the believer, regulating moral behavior, daily and social. The traditional commentator
gave the truth a transcendent dimension, an Islamic dimension, in a
culture that as we have seen constantly links religion and the secular
world (*din wa dunya*). This is an inevitable feature in a religious book
like the Qur'an that has both a practical and a social relevance.

TA'WIL: THAT IS HERMENEUTICS

Some Islamic thinkers are thus not limited to examining the formal
details of the text. The use of *ta'wil*, in rational or esoteric hermeneutics, is suggested in the Qur'an itself in the fundamental verse 3.7:
"It is He that has revealed to you the Book. And in it there are
clear (*muhkamat*) verses . . . and metaphorical (*mutashabihat*)". The
rendition of the term *mutashabihat* present some difficulties. Bausani translates it as "allegories". But the allegorical (one of the four
methods of interpretation of the sacred text, including the literal, the
moral and the analogical) means rather what remains beyond the

literal sense, but not in a controversial manner. It is interesting to note that Bonelli as well as Arberry and Abdel Haleem translate it as "ambiguous", and the sense of the Qur'anic text is really to suggest something ambiguous, not clear but rather difficult. However, if we are looking for a middle position, I prefer "metaphorical" since metaphor can reproduce or not reproduce what is metaphoricized. We follow the Qur'an here: "How many of those who go awry follow that which they regard as metaphorical, desiring to communicate anarchy and to interpret [according to their judgment] *(ta'wil)* while true interpretation *(ta'wil)* is only with *God Men are well founded in knowledge say*: We believe in this book, it comes entirely from Our Lord". The phrase in italics is awkward in English, but that is intended. The original Qur'anic text does not have punctuation. The phrase can be read in two ways, both valid: (1) the interpretation where knowledge is only with *God. Men who are well based in knowledge say* . . . ; (2) the interpretation where knowledge is only with *God and men are well founded in science. They say* . . . The difference is fundamental because in the first case it is suggested that only one person possesses knowledge of the secret and of how to interpret and that is God, while in the second case it suggests that, other than God, such an ability to understand is possessed "by men well based in science". Who are they supposed to be?

Al-Tabari has argued for the validity of the first version of the reading of the verse cited above: the interpretation of ambiguous passages is only with God, and also, as we have already seen, according to him the ambiguous and allegorized passages are very few, and the majority of verses are "solid" *(muhkamat)*. The solid verses are "those strengthened with clarity and detail" and their interpretation is easy for the *'ulama'*, the doctors of Law, those who are taken to coincide with the "well founded in science". Averroes, the celebrated philosopher from Andalus who commentated on Aristotle, has naturally found support (in the *Decisive Treatise*) for this quality in the philosophers and used the second version of the reading of verse 3.7: the interpretation of ambiguous passages is reserved for God *and* the philosophers. Averroes (2001: 10, 12, 20, 27) differentiates between four levels of reader of the text along the lines of a philosophical structure:

a. no metaphorical or allegorical interpretation is possible whenever it could go against the certain premises of a certain conclusion.

These are the axioms in such syllogisms, and the reasonings that take place in the "solid" verses of the sacred text deal with aspects of religions that cannot be challenged or put in doubt, such as the existence of God and his Unity, the existence of Paradise and Hell, the indubitability of the Day of Judgment, and so on;

b.   a metaphorical or allegorical interpretation is possible when it goes against certain premises to symbolic conclusions;

c.   a metaphorical or allegorical interpretation is possible about premises generally believed but not certain from which they result in certain conclusions;

d.   a metaphorical and allegorical interpretation is *obligatory* for people who are well based in knowledge, like the philosophers, and results in symbolic conclusions. There is a duty to prohibit completely the public as a whole from participation in *ta'wil*.

Averroes does not suggest examples through which we could examine his reasoning, but it is interesting to compare his breakdown of the four kinds of clarity expressed in the sacred Book with those arranged by al-Suyuti, a more traditional thinker and certainly not a philosopher:

The *'ulama'* divide up the Qur'an according to the level of semantic clarity, into four categories:

1.   the passages that are clear; they have only one possible sense and that is found in the text;

2.   the passages that have two meanings, of which one is preponderant (stronger) and the other secondary (probable) and that represents what is apparently the case, that which is open (*zahir*);

3.   the passages that can be allowed to have two meanings of equal probability that make up together a synthesis;

4.   the passages that are seen to have two meanings of unequal probability, where the preponderant meaning (the stronger) is not close to the text (the apparent meaning) as in the case of the second category, but the meaning is a long way from the text and that determines how it is interpreted.

(al-Suyuti quoted in Abu Zayd 1999: 184–185)

The first category of al-Suyuti clearly corresponds to point (a) of Averroes in denying any possible metaphorical or allegorical interpretation, just as the fourth category corresponds to point (d) of Averroes, suggesting the obligation to interpret metaphorically or allegorically. There are clear texts (the "solid" verses) that do not admit of any rational interpretation or really stick to the literal sense of the text. There are some texts with a plurality of meanings (the metaphorical or "ambiguous" verses) that provide the basis for such an interpretation. The smooth convergence between a rationalist philosophy like that of Averroes and a traditionalist commentator like al-Suyuti is perhaps rather significant. Naturally, we may infer that al-Suyuti attributes to the traditional commentators, to which class he himself belongs, the qualification of being "well based in knowledge". In any case, the interpretative enterprise is a lawful activity for both of them, and the verse 3.7 makes the obvious point, implicitly encouraging the speculative approach.

This fact is just as clear to the medieval scholars as it is to the modern. Baljon for example writes: "Like [before him] al-Zamakhshari, some of the modernists allot to the mutashabihat [ambiguous or metaphorical verses] the merit of inciting to study, or to put it shortly in the words of [the Qur'anic commentator] Ahmad al-Din: 'The Koran-verses which relate to fact (*haqiqat*) are exact (*muhkam*), and those which are the object of investigation (*tahqiqat*) are not clear (*mutashabihat*)'" (Baljon 1968: 52). The question is to decide on what level it is possible to pursue the investigation. In effect, the possible options are diverse and can leave us in something of a difficulty. Leah Kinberg has correctly noted how the term *mutashabihat* means not only "ambiguous" but also "simile", in that it is more appropriate to attribute to the verses in question the meaning of "metaphorical" as we have done. There exist, however, verses that are univocal, the "solid" ones, and verses like the *mutashabihat* that resemble them and reject both categories of interpretation.

From this point of view, as is immediately evident, we have come to confirm the inimitability of the Qur'an. The verses are mostly entirely solid. When they are ambiguous, *mutashabihat*, however, they have a parallel in other clear verses because in the Sacred Book there cannot be any possible contradiction. Thus the text provides evidence of its inimitability and miraculous construction. In this case, what are the limits of interpretative legitimacy? If the text is perfect and inimitable, ought we not to take it always in its literal sense? On this Kinberg suggests: "[T]he medieval commentators on the muhkamat and the mutashabihat ought to have concentrated all the light of the great polemic on the legitimacy of the interpretation of the Qur'an. [. . .] This phenomenon could lead to two contradictory conclusions: a) the flexibility of interpretation would lead people astray, with the conclusion that all interpretive activity ought to be prohibited; b) the flexibility of interpretation is a specific virtue of the Qur'an. Thanks to this virtue, the Qur'an serves as a source of responses and solutions to all problems at all times and in its turn was considered as one of the central characteristics of its miraculous nature" (Kinberg 1988: 164–165). The dialectical potential that exists between a "total interpretation" and a "limited interpretation" is really in the end rigorously circumscribed by the Book and plays a major role in contemporary Qur'anic enquiry, as we shall see in the next chapter.

Analyzing verse 3.7, Shiite theologians like al-Kulayni and al-Qummi have obviously argued that the "men well founded in knowledge" are the imams who followed 'Ali, to whom we should look for the symbolic interpretation of the holy text, its ta'wil. In this way interpretation is not limited to a linguistic or lexical investigation but inevitably assumes rational and spiritual aspects that can be found in an esoteric hermeneutics. In this case it is not so much looking for ambiguity in the verse, as it is the necessity of going beyond the literal sense in search of an allegorical or moral sense. Symbolic interpretation is potentially esoteric and a characteristic of Shiite theology controlled by the strong connections between imams and the sacred text. In general for the Shiites the imams have the ability to represent and clarify the arcane and secret meaning of Scripture, where the prophets, and Muhammad among them, are bearers of exoteric laws. The sixth imam Ja'far al-Sadiq (d. 765) said: "God has made our [the imam's] authority the pole of the Qur'an and the pole of all Scripture. To show this we turn to the 'solid' (muhkamat) verses of the Qur'an. Through it the Scriptures are said to be reflected and faith made manifest". Thus the imams possess complete knowledge of the secrets of the Qur'an and represent the Qur'an "talking" (natiq), while the Qur'an written down after the death of Muhammad became the "silent" (samit) Qur'an, which made interpretation compulsory. The esoteric law of Muhammad is "silent" with respect to all esoteric interpretation of the imams. The presupposition of this conception is that the sacred Text has two levels, one exterior (zahir) and one esoteric (*batin*). Naturally, the inner is the authentic level of explication, which divulges the secrets of divine truth, and the imams are those in receipt of it.

Shiism (or at least the Twelver form of imami Shiism) developed a science of traditional commentary based on authority. These are the already mentioned al-Qummi (d. 939), the famous al-Sayyid al-Murtada (d. 1044), and his disciples al-Tabarsi (d. 1153) and later on Muhammad al-Kashi (d. around the beginning of the sixteenth century), author of *Clarity in the Interpretation of the Qur'an*, which concentrates particularly on the study of the Traditions. Esoteric hermeneutics has brought with it a proliferation of mystical Qur'anic commentators, some of whom have been integrated by commentators in the classical sense, such as Rashid al-Din al-Maybudi (d. 1126), who defended an approach to the text that involved seven spiritual levels, according to the report of a hadith (authentic?) attributed to Muhammad. Henry Corbin, one of the greatest Western scholars of Shiism, has reported that the personalities such as al-Simnani (d. 1336), Molla Sadra Shirazi (d. 1640) or Abu'l-Hasan 'Amili Isfahani (d. 1726) composed treatises of gnostic hermeneutics that specified spiritual grades. Corbin is highly obsessive in his desire to find at all costs in Islam esoteric aspects, even at the cost of distorting the texts, on which he cannot always be trusted. But certainly esoteric investigation occupies a central role in Shiism, especially of the Isma'ili variety. The Isma'ilis, like all the Shiites, accepted the fundamental distinction between the exterior or the literal (*zahir*), and the interior or esoteric (*batin*), but have contributed to the traditional authoritative commentary tradition, although theologians like the judge al-Nu'man (d. 947) and Abu Ya'qub al-Sijistani (who lived in the tenth century) insisted on esoteric commentary. In any case, the Isma'ilis accepted exoteric revelation, which in technical terms is called the "descent" (*tanzil*), without which any esoteric enquiry cannot be started. The Prophet brought the revealed message and the Laws, and, as Muhammad said, he received the "descent" but designated a successor, an heir, who could interpret the Laws in an esoteric way. In the case of Muhammad this was 'Ali. Moses, the exoteric prophet, witnessed his deputy and interpreted this esoterically, and it was Aaron. A similar event saw Jesus with Simon Peter. It is obvious that, given these presuppositions, one can arrive at the conclusion that the deputy or heir is superior to the Prophet.

THE ABROGATOR AND THE ABROGATED

The science of abrogating (*nasikh*) and of the abrogated (*mansukh*) is particularly well developed in Islam and of extreme importance in establishing the definitive content of the Qur'an and its interpretation. It also defines the agreement between law and the Book. The doctrine essentially is to work out which verses of the Book, those that come chronologically later, cancel other prescriptions, or other verses chronologically earlier. This is done without admitting that there are contradictions or incoherence in the behavior of God, who abrogates some verses and supports better verses in order to perfect and bring to completion his revelation. Muslims identify in 2.106 the text that makes it clear that this *sunna* or customary disposition of God should spur us to study which verses abrogate which others: "We do not abrogate a verse or cause it to be forgotten without replacing it with something better or similar". This is what can be called "the abrogation of the Qur'an by the Qur'an" and constitutes a science that deals with the abrogation of the Qur'an by the *sunna*, the abrogation of the *sunna* by the Qur'an, with such a variety of alternatives that it is impossible to discuss them extensively here. In the course of the evolution of Islamic culture, the abrogation of the Qur'an by the Qur'an has taken on a rather less significant role to that of the abrogation of the Qur'an by the *sunna* or the *sunna* by the Qur'an.

As in every discipline that is part of the Islamic religion, the opinions of the scholars are more varied and sometimes opposed to each other on which verses can abrogate and which and how far others abrogate them. For example some have argued that the Qur'an at 3.7 calls "solid verses" (*muhkamat*) verses to be abrogators, and "metaphorical verses" (*mutashabihat*) the abrogated verses. But agreement is far from being unanimous. Most exegetes hold that 3.85 ("whoever chooses [a religion] different from Islam, it will not be accepted") abrogates 2.62 ("those who believe, whether they be Jews, Christians or Sabians . . . have their reward in our Lord"), but some authors have argued on the other hand that both verses are "solid". In any case, the doctrine of abrogation (*naskh*) brings into the text an apparent historical criterion. However, it is not right to base historicity on chronology, since historicity accepts that some prescriptions lose value due to being superseded by diverse circumstances.

This fact naturally leads us to consider the science of "circumstances" or "causes of revelation" (*asbab al-nuzul*), which is the science of when, how and why a verse was revealed; how rules lead us to determine which abrogates which; and what remains abrogated. Also in this case the opinions of the experts are not unanimous, and it has been said that there are only 42 abrogated verses, but some have selected 240 verses in this category. The proliferation over time of the number and type of abrogated verses and those that abrogate others has been defended by David Powers: "The rapid growth of the number is mirrored, I think, by two main factors. In the first place, the doctrine of abrogation needs to be invoked, since after the death of Muhammad all scope for reconciling the discrepancies that had been produced between the Qur'an and the fiqh [positive law] had otherwise disappeared. [. . .] In the second place—and more importantly—the expansion of the semantic scale of terms is said to include phenomena which originally did not fall under its ambit: [. . .] 'to replace one legal rule with another . . . specifications, exceptions, to abandon a legal rule because the circumstances have changed, reciprocal cancellation'" (Powers in Rippin 1988: 122–123). Andrew Rippin, extreme as often, has argued that the science of *asbab al-nuzul* is in the end a mystification. The origins of the causes of revelation are connected with the aim of those very causes. The commentators produced, so to speak, the causes of revelation in order to make internally consistent and coherent the Scripture that they—these same commentators—were producing accordingly. It is true, among other things, that the proliferation of cases of abrogation has long preoccupied Muslim scholars, and a later thinker like al-Suyuti has identified only twenty cases, those that are very easy to recognize as possible legal prescriptions, in which to speak effectively of abrogation.

The science of abrogated and the abrogating developed, so to say, "from without" the Qur'an, given the large number of times it was necessary to resolve incongruences in the text and incongruences between revelation and daily practical legal practice. That makes it difficult to argue that the results of the science are always entirely systematic, as some "fundamentalist" contemporary thinkers seem to think. We cite two examples. The first deals with the well-known prohibition of consuming alcohol and especially wine. In the early times of Muhammad's revelations, the consumption of alcoholic drinks seems to have been made legal. The Meccan verse 16.67 in fact states: "Of the fruits of the palm and the vine you obtain intoxicating drink [*sakar*, what the exegetes say is *khamr* or wine], and in this there is a sign for those who know". There follows a Medinan verse where the Qur'an seems to argue that such consumption is undesirable, but not entirely wrong: "They ask you about wine (*khamr*) and *maysir* [a sort of game of chance]. Say, in it there is great sin, but also some benefit for men" (2.219). Other verses, though all Medinan, abrogate this corrective and impose in a decisive manner a ban on intoxicating drink in order to save us from being tempted by demoniacal temptations: "In truth, wine, gambling, idols and arrows [for divination] are an abomination, the work of Satan" (5.90). It may be that the motive for this revelation was necessary because a number of Muslims tended to go to the mosque for prayers in a state of distraction or drunkenness. Very many Muslims are entirely rigorous in respecting these Qur'anic prescriptions, but there are some of them who maintain that the prohibition is not absolute but prohibits only excess that leads to intoxication.

The problem of wine is not very important from an authentic religious perspective. But when we come to war, the question of abrogation of a revealed text because of another text revealed perhaps later comes to take a central role. We will give just one example. Sura 16 (The Bee), which is Meccan and not the last revelation of Mecca, proves that in the confrontation with the unbelievers there should be a peaceful settlement and suggests placing any such confrontation on a level of discussion and moral suasion: "Those who do not believe in the Hereafter, they have stubborn hearts and are arrogant. [. . .] If you want to guide them [on the right path], however, God does not guide [them] and he makes them [go astray]. [. . .] Call all men to the way of the Lord with wisdom and good persuasion and dispute with them in the better way" (16.22, 37, 125). Sura 9 (Repentance) is Medinan and according to the Vulgate of Fu'ad is the penultimate one to have been revealed. It is much more aggressive: "Fight those who do not believe in God and in the Last Day and do not call illicit what God and his Messenger have called illicit, and those who have been given a Book, but do not practice the religion of Truth. Fight them until they pay the tribute and are overcome" (9.29). It is relevant to find out also which verses are chronologically closer to each other. For instance, the so-called "verse of the sword" (9.5: "Kill the idolaters [*mushrikun*] wherever you find them. Seize them, surround them, lie in wait for them") abrogates a verse that is equally bellicose but more restrained: "Fight in the way of God those who fight you, but do not go to extremes for God does not love those who go to extremes [this could also have been translated: do not aggress for God does not love those who aggress]" (2.190). Now, some experts have calculated that the "sword verse" abrogates 124 preceding verses. Otherwise, the clause on suspending the struggle and releasing the pagans if they convert and pay a tithe is contained in the second part of the already quoted verse 9.5, so some have argued that 9.5 abrogates itself and that this is a marvelous indication of the perfection of the Qur'an.

In general if it is argued that the later suras abrogate the first, or that a determinate number of verses abrogate others having a substantially similar content, it is evident that the incitement to struggle and to war abrogates the demand for dialogue and spiritual confrontation, and that the demand for struggle and war without mercy abrogates the demand for struggle carried out within certain limits. This fact has strongly conditioned the attitude of contemporary radical Muslims, like the already quoted Sayyid Qutb, who became, with the passage of the years, more intransigent and opposed to compromise. The facts involved in sorting out how to apply the doctrine of abrogated and abrogator match each other as far as the evidence is concerned, so radical Muslims can use the doctrine to justify the choice of their armed struggle. Obviously, open-minded thinkers like Nasr Abu Zayd contested the effectuality of abrogation aware of its dangerous implications.

THE MECCAN QUR'AN AND THE MEDINAN QUR'AN ACCORDING TO RECENT INTERPRETATIONS

It is possible that the content of the text has different levels of cogency. This is how it is taken by many Muslims. The differentiation between the Meccan and the Medinan Qur'an has intrigued and affected prospective theorists as well as Muslim militants. Did the Medinan Qur'an modify the Meccan Qur'an? Muhammad Mahmud Taha (1909–1985) thought that the Meccan Qur'an presented the eternal message from God for all humanity, while the Medinan Qur'an contains the contingent message revealed by God to Muhammad for the period of the new Islamic community. According to Taha, the more recent part of the Qur'an, the Medinan, does not abrogate the older part, the Meccan. In some ways he makes an obvious point here. The Meccan Qur'an, the older, constitutes the heart of the revelation, while the Medinan Qur'an, the more recent, was revealed in specific historical circumstances.

Taha has argued that the Meccan Qur'an is the Qur'an of the "Muslims" (*al-muslimun*), the universal Qur'an (all monotheists are Muslims, on this account), and he provides evidence that Islam is a natural religion (30.30), a revelation for all humanity. By contrast the Medinan Qur'an is the Qur'an of the "believers" (*al-mu'minun*), specifically those in a particular community. As Taha puts it:

> It is the duty of the inheritors of Islam, the inheritors of the Qur'an, to proclaim the Second Message in anticipation of the new era for which humanity feels a desperate need and to which it is unable to find the way. The way is the Qur'an, which of course does not speak: men must speak for it. God says in this connection "It (the Qur'an) is clear signs in the hearts of those who are given knowledge, and none but the unfair ones deny Our signs".
>
> (29.49)

> The phrase "the hearts of those who are given the knowledge" points the way to the new era, the way of the Muslimin on Earth as laid down in the primary texts of the Qur'an, those revealed in Mecca, which were repealed or abrogated during the first stage of Islam by the subsidiary texts—those revealed in Medina. The primary texts were abrogated then because of the dictates of the time (*hukm al-waqt*), as it was the time for the notion of Mu'minin. The primary texts address the nation of Muslimin, which did not come into being in that time.
>
> The primary texts were repealed or abrogated, in the sense of being postponed, and suspended in relation to legislation until their proper time, which has dawned upon us now. That is why we have applied ourselves to the proclamation of the Second Message
>
> (Taha 1987: 36–37)

Now, this proclamation has universal value, it transcends time, and the Meccan Qur'an can contribute to the construction of a new society based on the principles of Islam. Building on this point

Taha arrives at the conclusion that the normal prescriptions of the Medinan Qur'an are inadequate in modern society, being really the product of an historical necessity and so needing to be contextualized. It is hardly surprising that similar theses have been condemned by traditionalists, in particular the Muslim Brothers, but it is a matter of fact that in the Medinan phase of his life, Muhammad was at the same time both a prophet and a statesman, the bearer of the word of God and yet also the wise organizer of the community.

Sayyid Qutb has produced a distinctive theory of the relationship between the Medinan and the Meccan Qur'an, and his perspective is different from that of Taha. It is worth quoting a recent critic, Oliver Carré:

> The Medinan Quran announces just one thing: God is one and man is at his service. Nothing else: no national Arab program, nor social, military, legal or anything moral. The Meccan Qur'an is nothing else than a revolution (*thawra*) of conscience and belief, to establish first everything that follows: ethics, the state, laws, social order. [. . .] In brief, all sura 6, according to Qutb, all the Meccan Qur'an, is concentrated on faith (*'aqida*), not on law (*shari'a*), but it is relevant to legislation in this basis, since a fact of faith (*'aqida*) has profound implications for shari'a, law, in a future Islamic state. [. . .] The "Meccan Revolution", according to Qutb, is the imperative to *'ibada* [worship], that consists in the steadfast choice to not serve anyone except God, and to forbid serving anyone except Him. [. . .]

> For Qutb, the Medinan Qur'an is quite different, in both its content and intention, from the Meccan, but maintains the exemplary unified character of a primitive community. On the Medinan suras Qutb applies particularly the "dynamic tafsir", vital and combative. [. . .] This dynamic and vital Qur'an consists in "Qur'anic direction of life which has effectively taken place one day on this Earth" and "this Qur'anic life was the daily fact for Muslims mobilized for the perennial battle of the epoch". [. . .] All sura 2 [which is Medinan] is the effective elaboration of the exposition of the constitution and law of Islamic society. At Medina was realized "the highest and purest loyal society based on love and mutual cooperation".

(Carré 1984: 46–48)

The difference between the positions of Taha and Qutb are substantial: while that of Taha is a utopian perspective that results in the realization of a future society in which finally Islam will be the religion of true Muslims (*muslimun*), the perspective of Qutb is anti-utopian and sees in the society of Medina the realization on Earth, once for everyone, of the authentic Islamic state, inspired and in line with the word of God. The difference is not without importance for a judgment of the attitude of Muslims toward politics and the future state, and the Qur'an provides a way of resolving this issue.

THE SCIENCES OF THE QUR'AN ACCORDING TO AL-GHAZALI

In the period "of the concealment" (1095–1106) when he had abandoned public teaching and cultivated in solitude the spiritual life, al-Ghazali wrote a breviary as an introduction to the Qur'an with the purpose of demonstrating that the sacred Book contains the principles of all the sciences that the believer ought to practice to interpret the text. In this book, called *The Pearls of the Qur'an*, the theologian describes the sciences of the Qur'an and their reciprocal hierarchy by making use of a metaphor. The whole of the sciences is structured in a similar mode to a seashell that contains a pearl. The seashell represents exterior knowledge, the pearl its inner meaning. In a shell there is a skin on the outside and a side closer to the pearl; as with a pearl there is a surface and a kernel. Now, according to al-Ghazali, the skin that is outside the seashell, the more superficial skin, is the phonetic knowledge of how to read and to pronounce the Qur'an. The more internal science of the shell, what is around the pearl, is the science of traditional commentary (*tafsir*). In the middle is a science like that of recitation and grammar. The sciences of the shell, as we saw, are all linguistic. The science that exists entirely outside the pearl is that of the stories and the history of the prophets. On a very similar level come dialectical theology or *kalam* and jurisprudence. The sciences of the kernel of the pearl, the fundamental sciences, are, in an ascending order of importance, the science of acts, that of attributes and finally that of the essence of God. This classification and hierarchical structure demonstrates evidently how al-Ghazali sees the interpretation of the text as a process of evolution toward a level that is always more esoteric. But esoterism does not necessarily mean, in his view, the gnostic and spiritual hermeneutics (*ta'wil*) of the Isma'ilis, although they also make a distinction between the exoteric (*zahir*) and the interior (*batin*). Esoterism he sees as the Qur'anic science of the essence of God imposing a route through the exterior language of the text to the understanding of the secret theology that the text contains to whoever knows how to interpret it. According to N. Heer (1993), for al-Ghazali we can use reason to work out which verses ought to be interpreted metaphorically; interpretation is the result of an illuminative "development" (*mukashafa*), and so there can be no contradiction between the esoteric and the exoteric.

In this sense it is perhaps possible to say that the major work of al-Ghazali, the *Revivification of the Religious Sciences*, constitutes a commentary on the Qur'an and develops systematically in the articulation of his books an enquiry into the sciences of the Qur'an. This approach is repeated by the author in two of his other writings (and it is not important to determine their chronology): the *Pearls of the Qur'an* and *Forty Principles of Religion*. In the *Pearls of the Qur'an*, al-Ghazali finds in the sacred Book two great groups of revelations, the first relates to the "sciences" (*'ilm*) and the second to "actions" (*'amal*). Knowledge and action can be considered by theology the fundamental themes of the Qur'an. What belongs to the first group, knowledge, are ten themes derivable from the Qur'an and from the study of tradition (quoted in the *Pearls of the Qur'an*: in the other two writings the specification undergoes some variations or some resystematization of order, but remains more or less the same): the essence of God, his holiness, his power, his knowledge, his will, his hearing and sight, his Word, his acts, the Day of Judgment and Prophecy.

For the second group, that of action, belong a good thirty themes (al-Ghazali nurtures a strong ethical and practical interest) subdivided into "exterior acts" that are those acts of religion prescribed by Law, "blameworthy acts" from which the soul ought to be cleansed, and finally "praiseworthy acts" that are indispensable for following the mystical and spiritual path and reaching God. These are the exterior acts: prayer, prescribed charity, fasting, pilgrimage to Mecca, recitation of the Qur'an, mentioning the names of God, discovering what is lawful, right behavior, commending the good and forbidding evil, and following the *sunna* of the Prophet. Much of the essence and acts of God make up this form of knowledge, such as the profession of faith and the five principles that are obviously sanctified by the Qur'an. Studying and applying them means to study and apply the

Qur'an. Bad behavior and the praiseworthy are general moral rules or specific stages of the soul that are not present in the Qur'an in such quantities. To avoid the illicit and to control the passions, on the one hand, and to foster fear, patience and trust in God, on the other, are aspects of the divine decree. All meditation on death leads to instruction in morality that naturally has a textual basis since the sacred text is very much a code of ethical behavior.

THE SCIENCES OF THE QUR'AN ACCORDING TO TRADITIONALIST AUTHORS

Al-Ghazali was an intellectual who could wonderfully synthesize theology with philosophy and mysticism with law. The taxonomy of knowledge in the Qur'an fitted in well with his analytical and theoretical interests and also with his spirituality. Jalal al–Din al–Suyuti—author of a famous manual on the science of the Qur'an, the *Kitab al-iqtan fi 'ulum al-Qur'an* (The refinement of knowledge of the Qur'an)—moves along a landscape that is apparently more prosaic and dry, but the work distilled centuries of traditional exegeses and is a veritable encyclopedia that gives us information about hundreds of authors and texts. The knowledge of the Qur'an that he explains is the usual one: the distinction between the Meccan and Medinan Qur'an, the various kinds of revelation, the "cause" or "circumstance" of revelation, how the Qur'an should be memorized and recited, the solid and the metaphorical verses, the abrogated and the abrogating, inimitability and so on. With respect to all knowledge of commentary, al-Suyuti analyzed the various opinions of the experts, from which emerge the tendency of commentators to consider *tafsir* as something more general and a bit more superficial than *ta'wil*. The Egyptian polymath said that *tafsir* is "clarificatory" and "progressive", while *ta'wil* is a "return" (closer to sources and roots) because "it occupies itself with the meanings that the verses have" (Suyuti n.d.: vol. II, 221ff.). The *tafsir* by contrast is limited to detail, while *ta'wil* explains.

From a certain point of view, the results obtained by al-Suyuti in what we call the "Middle Ages" turned out to be definitive. The contemporary exegete Subhi al-Salih, in his *Research on the Science of the Qur'an* (published for the first time in 1959), does not seem to go beyond certain limits. In the first part of the book, which is taken up with the rules of the Qur'an and its secrets, he provides arguments for theories such as revelation being one for all the prophets, although the Islamic revelation had its own specific properties. In the second part, mainly on the "sciences" of the Qur'an, he discusses the specific aspects of classical Islamic enquiry, such as the science of the "circumstances of revelation" (*asbab al-nuzul*), the distinction between the Meccan and Medinan Qur'an, the "suspended" letters, the science of recitation, that of abrogation, and the distinction between the "solid" and the "ambiguous" verses. In the last part, the question of the traditional commentary of *tafsir* and the inimitability of the Qur'an are discussed.

The formulation of entirely traditional approaches to explanation does not prevent other forms of interpretation going beyond the usual limits. Some comments scattered around Subhi al-Salih can point to new ways of reflection. However, the author supports the position that the sacred Book exhibits a gradual evolution of legislation (*tadarruj al-tashri'*). This is not merely a repetition of what has already been said on the relationship between the abrogated and the abrogating verses but refers to a highly evolved concept of law, in the light of a universal motivating principle: that of the (golden) mean. Subhi al-Salih writes that Islam wished to preserve balance and the balance of the Umma with a variety of believers, and between religious and social acts. A theme, and an important one, of Muslim culture is this point that other radical authors such as Sayyid Qutb have affirmed—that Islamic is by nature far from all excess.

In the second place, he discussed criteria with which to distinguish the chapters from Mecca and those from Medina. Subhi al-Salih selects four elements that securely classify a sura as Medinan: (a) the authorization of *jihad*, where this is armed struggle against the pagans and the evildoers; (b) detail on issues dealing with the penal code, laws and duties, and civil, social and international legislation; (c) references to "hypocrites" who may be pretending to have been converted or to be allied with the Muslims and are in reality obstacles to the Prophet's mission; (d) the doctrinal dispute against the people of the Book (Jews and Christians) and the invitation to them to turn away from their excesses in their extreme religious views (such as belief in the Trinity, for example). The choice, in the Medinan Qur'an, of prevailing normative elements, as much on the level of military factors as on the level of legislation and propaganda, seems to distinguish it according to Subhi from the Meccan (a point already made by Taha), while naturally Subhi does not push the Medinan text as having a distinctive significance as opposed to the Meccan.

In the third place, the author, analyzing the famous distinction between the "solid" and the "ambiguous" verses states in a tentative manner that the Qur'an contains verses that are ambiguous (*mutashabihat*) and not only solid verses (*muhkamat*) since they are supposed to stimulate all people to deepen and study what knowledge they can gather of the interpretation of expressions that are not clear in the sacred Book, while, from another point of view, the Qur'an is all "solid", being "a Book in which signs are solid and precise" (11.1). It is interesting to have stressed the significant potential of the text being resuscitated in its pure meaning as having a "structure" that is sufficient by itself to carry out the function that it enunciates.

THE AUTHENTICITY OF THE QUR'AN

We have spoken a lot in the second chapter on the structure and the "composition" of the Qur'an, on the dating of the text, on the language in which it has been written, here on the abrogated and the abrogating, but nothing much yet on the burning issue of the authenticity of the Qur'an. Whether the Qur'an is authentic is well beyond doubt for the believer, but the question of authenticity constitutes a fundamental aspect of scientific research on the text. Naturally, in Islamic Studies as carried out by European or American orientalists, there is no lack of argument that the Qur'anic text is the result of a pious fraud with which the generations following Muhammad wished to find a transcendent basis in the teaching of the Prophet, and that it is a collection and systematization of pre-existing traditions. John Wansbrough has sought to show that the Qur'an acquired much of its definitive form in the second century after the death of Muhammad and is based on collections of reports whose authenticity is in many cases very dubious. He was joined by Patricia Crone and Michael Cook who have written: "There is no decisive evidence that the Qur'an existed in any form before the last decade of the seventh century: and the tradition which puts this opaque revelation in its historical context is not seen first until the middle of the eighth century" (Crone and Cook 1977: 3). Andrew Rippin (2001) has connected the "falsification" of the Qur'an with exegetical activity, since the activity of the "formation" of the text and the activity of its interpretation are really parallel. Revisionism about the sources of Islam, inspired by authors like Wansbrough and Crone, have been built into a system in a study by Daniel Brown, *A New Introduction to Islam*. In the reconstruction of Brown, the traditional accounts of Arab and Muslim authors of Mecca at the time of Muhammad are fantasies. The life of the Prophet is historically dubious in the way in which it is reported in later stories, and the hadith are substantially false. It is certainly the case that the text and its history needs to be discussed, especially given its antiquity. Brown puts it rather drily: "[T]he history of the birth of Islam in Arabia seems implausible because it is an implausible fact" (Brown 2004: 17).

These revisionist theses are fundamentally based upon the (true) fact that endogenous Islamic sources about the composition of the Book and the life of the Prophet are chronologically late, written sometimes a couple of centuries after the narrated facts. The strong point of the Wansbrough-Crone-Cook thesis consists in the fact that we do not possess Muslim sources from the same time or a little after the relevant facts, while an "Islamic" literature emerged in the absence of such witnesses from the beginning of the eighth century. I recognize that this is true, but many orientalists approached the question negatively with the bias that these sources, because late, are also false or mostly unreliable. It is a prejudice that has been challenged by other scholars. Neal Robinson, for example, has effectively contested the revisionist approach. He is quite right to point out, with many examples, that the non-Islamic sources that the revisionists use are far from being trustworthy and beyond critical question themselves. On the other side, the systematic undervaluation or devaluation of the Arab/Islamic source is equivalent to the systematic prejudicial negation of the verisimilitude of all the Christian sources relating to Jesus and the birth and growth of Christianity, which is a radical skepticism clearly without foundation. A more powerful point, in my opinion, is the argument, which we have already used, by Robinson that the structure of the Qur'anic text can be seen to obey an internal logic that is very precise and systematic that more genuine study can make evident. We have discussed widely the issue in Chapter 3 in this volume.

Recently, Fred Donner gave a substantial contribution to the discussion. First, he argued (Donner 1998) that the narratives of Islamic origins are more reliable than supposed by Wansbrough. Recently (Donner 2010) he argued that the Muslim community acquired the awareness to be "Muslim" very slowly, while at the beginning it included also Christian and Jews. Be this hypothesis true or not, it is however based on the traditional Islamic version of Muhammad's biography considered as reliable.

The problem is that, if the hypothesis of Wansbrough and others in his group would be true, it would serve to destroy the very basis of Islamic civilization in the light of philology and critical history. For a culture like that of Islam, in which the text takes on a sacred value that it seeks to display within the context of a book, this can be especially damaging. Many contemporary Muslim interpreters have grasped the contradiction between the necessity of admitting the authenticity of the received text and that of having to apply a modern historical/critical methodology. It is ironic to note that, if it is true that all the information about the origins and development of Islam and on the formation of the holy text are a noble lie, the fact is that, notwithstanding everything, Islam has succeeded and is spread around the world and expanded very far from its original roots. This might lead someone to conclude that it was due to a divine miracle and so provided an argument in favor of the Muslim revelation! In any case, to the skepticism of the orientalists, the Muslims have often replied with an apologetic defense of the authenticity of the Qur'an.

From a certain point of view, and this point of view remains to be determined, to ask if the Qur'an (like the Bible and the Gospels) is authentic is a futile question. What is important is that Muslims have for centuries acted, believed and lived on the basis of *this* Qur'an. What is important about the role and function of the Qur'an is that we possess what has undoubtedly been for centuries a turning point in the religious psychology on the inner spiritual path of the believer. Also, Islam is both a religion and a world, part of the civil and social history of the Islamic Community. In this sense, *the text possesses a value of objectivity that lies in something other than its authorship: the value of truth and of the objectivity of the text is independent of who wrote it, whether he [the writer] is God or he is a pious 'alim [scholar] as a few orientalists suggested*. It is acceptable to apply the philosophical hermeneutic perspective as developed by Hans Gadamer, saying that the text possesses an alterity or otherness with respect to the author and with respect to the interpreter. It lives an autonomous life, and

THE QUR'AN AND THE QUR'ANIC SCIENCES

as Umberto Eco puts it: "[T]he author ought to die after he has finished writing. In order not to disturb the journey of the text" (Eco 1986: 509). This implies that a holy text can be as autonomous from its author as a novel or some other literary work.

Regis Blachère, one of the most important of the Qur'anic scholars of the last century, recognizing the importance of establishing a critical edition of the Qur'an according to the criterion of the orientalists, and pointing out that such an edition would not represent the Vulgate, asked: "In what case is the study of the diversity useful to our knowledge of Islam within the framework of theology and law? Will we have a clearer idea if we conclude that, in a difficult passage, the reading taken from the Vulgate is problematic and that another reading that is not canonical ought to be substituted? It is not certain. In the end, generations of exegetes and jurists have based their doctrine on certain readings considered, rightly or wrongly, as unrevisable: what is the profit in the suggestion that they are mistaken? For the non-Muslim world, the important thing is not to be certain what it ought to be, but to know what it is, and to interpret it in the way the Muslim Community does it" (Blachère 1977: 197).

In any case, the fact that the means of writing down the Qur'an occurred so recently—about twenty years after the death of the Prophet, when the record of its impressions and its words were still so fresh (as we saw in Chapter 2 in this volume)—constitutes for the majority of Muslim scholars an evident proof of its authenticity. Not only did a large number of the companions of the Prophet remain alive and able to direct the works of the commission, but after such a short time since the disappearance of the bearer of the revelation it would be have been impossible to falsify. As the Pakistani Abu Ala al-Mawdudi (1903–1979) has argued, to doubt the authenticity of the Qur'an is to go against the logic of history; it is like doubting the existence of Napoleon. In the second place, according to al-Mawdudi, the authenticity of the Qur'an is demonstrated in its appearance in the old manuscripts of the Book (that were preserved in Kufic and without diacritics) and the modern editions with the backing they receive from official bodies (in the Muslim countries there are many of these) and the fact that some people who are completely illiterate know the text by heart. Moreover, there is the autonomy of the Qur'an with respect to the Hebrew Bible: in al-Mawdudi's view, a serious enquiry can demonstrate that the Qur'anic stories are quite independent from the biblical and that they correct many mistakes present in the biblical accounts.

The modern Egyptian philosopher Hasan Hanafi has argued that only the Islamic revelation of Muhammad has come to us verbatim, while the Jewish and Christian revelations, in the Bible and the Gospels, are the result of revelations that have only been "transmitted" and so may well have been distorted:

> The words uttered by the Prophet [were] dictated to him by God via the Holy Spirit and dictated by the Prophet to the scribes immediately at the time of uttering and conserved by writing till today. These words constitute the revelation in verbatim. They do not pass by a period of oral transmission, but were written at the same time as when they were uttered. No Scripture in the Biblical tradition fulfills this condition except the Qur'an. The Old Textament passed through centuries of oral transmission. The New Textament passed through a Century of oral transmission. Only the Qur'an was written at the time of its uttering. In the case of written transmission, these texts must contain literally the same words uttered by the Prophet. The passage from the oral transmission to the written must be done according to the rules of oral transmission. The texts have to be known. They have to be identical. Their narrators have to be contemporaries to the events reported and completely neutral in their narration. Taking Graf-Wellhausen as a model, the G,E,D,P, sources are not known. They do not fulfill the conditions of the written transmission. The sources behind these sources are more obscure (the fragments from tribal and local songs [song of Lamech, sites of Moab, song of the well, song of Heshbon and Sion], the curses and the blessings [of Noah, of Melchisedec, of Rebecca, of Jacob, of Esan, of Joseph . . .], the oracles [of Rebecca, of Moses], the national songs . . . etcetera).
>
> (Hanafi 1977: 5)

As we have seen, Hanafi puts in contention the basis of biblical tradition (overturning with his enquiry the doubts raised about the Qur'anic transmission) in the name of an authenticity of the Qur'an that is derived as much from the contemporaneity of the Prophet as with his drawing up of the document that has immediately linked the orality of the Scripture with the literality of the text.

SUMMARY

In this chapter we have dealt with

- The names of the Holy Book.
- The science of the Qur'anic commentary with the distinction between *tafsir*, the traditional commentary, and *taw'il*, properly the hermeneutical exegesis.
- The clear and the ambiguous verses along with the philosophical and scholastic interpretations of the subject.
- The science of abrogation and its consequences for the reading of the text.
- The difference between the Qur'anic readings of Sayyid Qutb and Mahmud Taha.
- The so-called "sciences of the Qur'an", discussing in particular al-Ghazali's and Subhi al-Salih's positions.
- The debates over the authenticity of the Qur'an, discussing in particular the revisionist school of John Wansbrough and his students and the challenges posed to them.
- The vindication of the authenticity of the Qur'an by contemporary Muslim scholars.

REFERENCES/READINGS

Abu Zayd, N. (Abou Zeid), *Critique du discours religieux*, Sindbad-Actes Sud, Arles 1999.

Averroes, *On the Harmony of Religion and Philosophy*, trans. G. Hourani, Luzac, London 1976.

Averroes, *Decisive Treatise and Epistle Dedicatory*, trans. C. Butterworth, Brigham Young University Press, Provo 2001.

Ayoub, M. *The Speaking Qur'an and the Silent Qur'an: A Study of the Principles and Development of Imami Shii Tafsir*, in A. Rippin (ed.), *Approaches to the History of the Interpretation of the Qur'an*, Clarendon Press, Oxford 1988, pp. 177–198.

al-Azami, M.M. *The History of the Qur'anic Text*, UK Islamic Academy, Leicester 2003.

Baljon, J.M.S. *Modern Muslim Koran Interpretation (1880–1960)*, Brill, Leiden 1968.

Blachère, R. *Introduction au Coran*, Maisonneuve, Paris 1977.

Brown, D.A. *New Introduction to Islam*, Blackwell, Oxford 2004.

Burton, J. *The Sources of Islamic Law: Islamic Theories of Abrogation*, Edinburgh University Press, Edinburgh 1990.

Carré, O. *Mystique et politique: Lecture Révolutionnaire du Coran par Sayyid Qutb*, Cerf, Paris 1984.

Corbin, H. *History of Islamic Philosophy*, Kegan Paul, London 1993.

Crone, P. and Cook, M. *Hagarism: The Making of the Islamic World*, Cambridge University Press, Cambridge 1977.

Donner, F. *Narratives of Islamic Origins: The Beginning of Islamic Historical Writing*, Darwin Press, Princeton 1998.

Donner, F. *Muhammad and the Believers: At the Origins of Islam*, Harvard University Press, Cambridge, MA 2010.

Eco, U. *Postille a "Il Nome della Rosa"*, Bompiani, Milano 1986.

Ennaifer, H. *Les Commentaires Coraniques Contemporains: Analyse de leur Méthodologie*, Pontificio Istituto di Studi Arabi e di Islamistica, Roma 1998.

Gätje, H. *The Qur'an and Its Exesegis*. Selected Texts. Routledge and Kegan Paul, London 1976.

al-Ghazali, *The Pearls of the Koran*, trans. M. Abul Quasem, Kegan Paul, London 1983 (Italian translation by M. Campanini, *Le Perle del Corano*, Rizzoli, Milano 2016).

Gilliot, C. *Exégèse, Langue et Théologie en Islam: L'Exégèse Coranique de Tabari*, Vrin, Paris 1990.

Hanafi, H. *Religious Dialogue and Revolution*, Anglo-Egyptian Bookshop, Cairo 1977.

Heer, N. Abu Hamid al-Ghazali's Exoteric Exegesis of the Koran, in AA. VV. (ed.), *The Heritage of Sufism: Classical Persian Sufism from its Origins to Rumi*, Oneworld, Oxford 1993, pp. 235–257.

Jalalayn, *Al-Qur'an al-karim bi'l-Tafsir al-Jalalayn*, Matba'a al-Anwar al-Muhammadiyya, Cairo n.d.

Kinberg, L. "Muhkamat and Mutashabihat (Koran 3:7): Implication of a Koranic Pair of Terms in Medieval Exegesis", *Arabica* XXXV, 1988, pp. 143–172.

Lagarde, M. *Index du Grand Commentaire de Fakhr al-Din al-Razi*, Brill, Leiden 1996.

Madigan, D. *The Qur'an's Self-Image*, Princeton University Press, Princeton 2001.

al-Mawdudi, A. *Towards Understanding the Qur'an,* edited by Zafar I. Ansari, The Islamic Foundation, Leicester 1998.

McAuliffe, J. Quranic Hermeneutics: The Views of al-Tabari and Ibn Kathir, in A. Rippin, *Approaches to the History of the Interpretation of the Qur'an*, Clarendon Press, Oxford 1988, pp. 46–62.

Powers, D. *The Exegetical Genre "nasikh al-Qur'an wa mansukhuhu"*, in A. Rippin, *Approaches to the History of the Interpretation of the Qur'an*, Clarendon Press, Oxford 1988, pp. 117–138.

Rippin, A. *Approaches to the History of the Interpretation of the Qur'an*, Clarendon Press, Oxford 1988.

Rippin, A. *The Qur'an and Its Interpretative Tradition*, Aldershot, Ashgate, 2001.

Robinson, N. *Discovering the Qur'an*, SMC Press, London 2003.

al-Salih, S. *Mabahith fi 'ulum al-Qur'an, (Researches on the Qur'anic Sciences)*, Dar al-Mallaiyyn, Beirut 2002.

Shah, M. (ed.), *Tafsir. Interpreting the Qur'an: Critical Concepts in Islamic Studies*, Routledge, London–New York 2012.

al-Suyuti, *Kitab al-Itqan fi 'ulum al-Qur'an*, 2 vol., Dar al-Ma'rifa, Beirut n.d.

Taha, M. *The Second Message of Islam*, Syracuse University Press, New York 1987.

Wansbrough, J. *Qur'anic Studies: Sources and Method of Scriptural Interpretation*, Oxford University Press, Oxford 1977.

Watt, W.M. and Bell, R. *Introduction to the Qur'an*, Edinburgh University Press, Edinburgh 1970.

5

CONTEMPORARY APPROACHES TO THE QUR'AN

ISLAM CONFRONTING MODERNITY

We have already seen in the first chapters of this book an account of the interpretation of the Qur'an, especially with reference to the solutions advanced in what we call the Middle Ages (which corresponds to the highest level of Islamic civilization). Now we are going to deal with the problem of interpretation in the contemporary age. The contemporary age (meaning in particular the twentieth century; the renaissance of the Islamic world can be said to have actually started in the eighteenth century) has seen a period of intense interpretive activity with respect to the Qur'an, no less significant than the "medieval" period. And this is for the good reason that, in the contemporary age, Muslims have had to deal with and respond to European civilization and culture, often labeled as modernity. This modernity can be described in various ways, in particular in terms of specific concepts that characterize European civilization and that are on many points contrary to traditional Islamic mentality and culture.

First there is secularism, the separation of the internal and the external, between religion and society (and especially between religion and politics). Islam, as we have noted many times, integrates religion and secular affairs and involves a holistic conception of reality, for which secularism, and especially radical secularism, appears to be entirely alien. Second, technology that has subdued nature and brought it under human control is now considered the connective point between nature and humanity. In Islam, wisdom is life, not power, and nature has to be helped (used for the benefit of everyone) and not forced to satisfy ends that are foreign to it. Third, the nation, democracy and natural rights are political categories that collide with classical concepts in Islamic political philosophy and jurisprudence like Umma (Community), caliphate and the origin of right in the will of God and in revelation. Finally, individualism appears to be in clear opposition to the leading collective and holistic character of Islam.

The dialectic with modernity has significance from a certain point of view, that of alienation, since modernity has imposed on Muslims the necessity to re-read, see again, judge, and think about correcting or better understanding the fundamental principles of their own culture to connect it up with a reality that seems likely to dominate and shatter the Islamic world. We recall that the triumph of European modernity for many decades meant the subordination of the Islamic world through colonialism and Western imperialism. And it was with respect to colonial occupation and wars of conquest that the Muslims have come to know modernity, and this could only have been traumatic. Without this encounter with modernity Muslims might well have remained closed in on themselves, secure in their spirit of superiority and self-sufficiency. One of the obvious ways to assess the chances of Islam surviving its encounter with modernity is by assessing the impact that modernity had on the study of its basic text, the Qur'an.

THE QUR'ANIC COMMENTARIES OF THE SALAFIYYA

The Salafiyya is a reformist movement of considerable energy that, created in the second half of the nineteenth century, has stimulated a renaissance of Islam, especially in the Arab world, and that reached its peak about the first half of the twentieth century. The initiator of Salafism could be taken to be the Persian Jamal al-Din al-Afghani (1839–1897), who worked for a long time in Egypt and Istanbul. The principal disciple of al-Afghani was Muhammad 'Abduh (1849–1905), mufti of Egypt and a famous teacher, one of the most significant intellectuals of the Arab world at that time. 'Abduh was linked more or less directly to the Syrian Rashid Rida (1865–1935) and to the Algerian 'Abd al-Hamid ibn Badis (1889–1940) and to many other thinkers who will not be discussed here. From many points of view, the reformist project of the Salafis represented the point of departure for the organization of the Muslim Brothers, founded in Egypt in 1928 by a teacher, Hasan al-Banna, which later on became embedded in all the countries of the Near East and North Africa.

The leading principles of the Salafiyya can be summed up in a few points: return to the original sources of Islam, renovating its customs from the point of view of a constant political and social reexamination, assimilation of science and modern knowledge, discovering for Islam and for the Arab people a role in history at a time when it was dominated by European colonialism. Salafism is certainly involved in Qur'anic commentary from the point of view of implementing these basic principles. According to H'mida Ennaifer (1998), the traditional Salafi commentators—among whom we can mention scholars such as the Tunisian Muhammad al-Tahir ibn 'Ashur (1879–1973) and the Iranian Shi'ite Muhammad Husayn Tabataba'i (1904–1981)—highlight some defects that have compromised the utility and the adequacy of their commentaries in the contemporary world. In summary, these defects are (a) maintaining internally the longstanding stability of the traditional order, so as to safeguard, with the unity of the text, the unity of the Community; (b) privileging the understanding of the Qur'an on the basis of the *sunna* (in other words, prioritizing what we have called commentary according to authority and tradition as opposed to rational commentary); (c) linking the interpretation of the text with the meaning encapsulated at the moment of revelation, which is to say, to magnify the sacred nature of the text and minimize its historical flexibility; (d) establishing the traditional commentaries, as given by ancient authorities, as, so to speak, "second texts" that have approximately the same authority and the same standing as the "first text", the Qur'an itself. These shortcomings, however, even if they can be found in the works of the later Salafi commentators, like Ibn 'Ashur and Tabataba'i, cannot be found in the commentaries of the first Salafi thinkers, like 'Abduh and Rida.

In fact, on their reformist project, 'Abduh and Rashid Rida both started, but did not complete, a huge Qur'anic commentary, the commentary of *Manar* (The Lighthouse), the name of a journal, edited by

Rida, in which the commentary was published in sections and then collected into a volume. Ibn Badis was essentially a preacher and a publicist, and his reflections on the Qur'an, systematic and profound but not really constituting a commentary as such, came out in the form of articles in another journal, *al-Shihab* (*The Meteor*). The aim of the Salafis was to describe the Qur'an as a rational construction in order to establish its value as a structure of thought, as a source of theological and moral teaching that can enable the Islamic people to confront modernity. In this sense, the role of the commentator (and of the commentary) is not irrelevant to the social and political context. The "construction" of the Qur'an has to be assessed by the ambiguous and slippery concept of rationality. It is difficult to say what is rationality, to give an absolutely philosophical definition that is univocal and precise. But the Salafis, 'Abduh especially, argued that Islam and the Qur'an are rational. 'Abduh maintains that the Qur'an is the only sacred text that argues in a rigorous demonstrative and deductive manner, that it is full of basic scientific remarks on humanity and the universe, and that Islam is the only religion that seeks to argue by rational proofs and can be used as the basis to further knowledge. This assumption runs throughout the whole commentary of the *Manar*. In many places it is suggested that faith, in Islam, is founded on reason. Having based itself on reason through demonstrative proof, faith provides believers with the means capable of mobilizing them and binding them to God and to His religion.

This fundamental rationalist attempt can be described on a number of levels. It is a strong critique of the principle of authority and slavish and blind imitation (*taqlid*). It deals with a common claim of Islamic reformers, from the time of Ibn Taymiyya (d. 1328) who sought to reopen the door to the autonomous and rational investigation of the principles of dogma and jurisprudence. There is, secondly, the claim—which is frequent enough in Islamic tradition, at least of the Sunni variety—that Islam is in fact a religion without mystery, especially as regards God. There is nothing to be revealed about God, no incarnation, no Trinity, no sacrament. The openness of God is guaranteed by the fact that the human mind is able to apply itself to science and nature. Hasan Hanafi (b. 1935) said that it is useless to speculate on the essence of God—the important thing is to struggle for the progress and liberation of humanity. So there is no room for the miracle that surprises and stupefies the naive, and conditions and distorts faith: "[I]n the commentary of Manar", states Jacques Jomier, "Shaykh 'Abduh insists on the fact that the miracle (*mu'jiza*) has an apologetic character and is used to support the credibility of revelation. He supports the idea, dear to Muslims, that the time of miracles (*mu'jiza*) is finite. Muhammad brought in the epoch of reason. Miracles were necessary at the time of the infancy of humanity. The Islamic faith, argued 'Abduh, rests on reason" (Jomier 1954: 159). This means that the Salafi condemn all superstitions such as Marabutism, the cult of saints, as aspects of popular religiosity. It is a rigorous approach that earlier Ibn Taymiyya and the puritan movement of the Wahhabis, in Arabia toward the end of the eighteenth century, had promoted. In response to credulity, the response is "philosophical". 'Abduh takes up Mu'tazilite positions to defend human free will and to appeal to natural causes as coming from the direct intervention of God (according to classical Islamic theology, such as the Ash'arite school, God creates the actions of humans, and nature functions only because God determines it continually). These are challenging and progressive theoretical positions. But we should not believe that 'Abduh and Rida were absolute rationalists. We can say that for both of them there is a sphere of knowledge unavailable to humanity and reserved for God only. Humanity is incapable, by itself, of attaining knowledge of everything. In his fundamental theoretical work, the *Letter on the Unity of God*, 'Abduh writes: "Islam frees reason of all its fetters and frees it from the imitations that have been applied to it, making it master of what it can rule on according to its judgment, and its wisdom. However, reason ought to bow to God only and stop at the limits of religion, since inside these limits there are no barriers to its activities".

The commentaries on the Qur'an and the reform activity have in the end the same purpose. They are designed to encourage the Muslim Community to reappraise its consciousness. The aim is not epistemological only but also to polemicize against their adversaries. Commenting on verse 3.19 ("religion [*din*] with God is Islam"), Rida comments that "the duty of the Muslim is not to insert the verse in the exposition of the annals of history, nor as the clue for the story of religions, nor in a polemical context, but to understand the verse remembering that it was revealed to give directives and provide lessons to those who believe. Man fears differences in religious matters, the breaking up into factions of sects and legal schools that have characterized preceding generations" (quoted in Jomier 1954: 111). This is because, in the words of Jacques Jomier, according to Rida "the Prophet came and the Qur'an was transmitted to guide humanity. A true commentary is that which reflects perfectly what Allah expects of men, the path on which he wishes to direct us. The commentary of *Manar* was more than anything else a commentary of 'directions'. The idea is expressed right at the beginning and runs throughout the whole of the twelve volumes" (Jomier 1954: 49).

Basically, the point of the *Manar* commentary is to defend religion from the possibility of accusations of obscurantism (naturally, from the point of view of scientific positivism that was widespread during that period): apologetics is the instrument to pursue practical and political action. Islam has no need to be modernized; it constitutes the universal response, eternally valid to questions that concern humanity, and also for the questions that can be raised within the ambit of science and technology. It is an apologetic point, and apologetics hinders an interpretation of the text in a philosophical sense. The scope for constructing the text is semantically limited to only one kind of meaning, and that is anti-utopian. Naturally, apologetics defends a certain vision of Islam, such as, for example, the fact that Islam is a religion of tolerance. We have already looked at verse 2.256 ("there is no compulsion in religion"). Rashid Rida has written that "faith is the expression of consent of the spirit. It is impossible for this consent to be extorted by coercion and constriction" (quoted in PISAI 1985: 17). In his turn, 'Abduh has affirmed dryly that Islam did not expand with the sword and violence. The affirmation is historically possible, but 'Abduh does not exemplify it by producing it clearly. The Salafi interpretation of *jihad* is that war is allowed, but only in response to aggression. *Jihad* has limits that are exclusively defensive, and it is this that is a collective duty. However, the commentators of the Salafiyya do not refrain from stressing that, in their time, the Muslim people were colonized and subjected to assault and wars, and this constitutes a huge contrast with the past, where, in the territories of Islam, the people of the Book, the Jews and the Christians, lived quietly and prospered due to their protected status.

Despite the existence of apologetics, the intention of 'Abd al-Hamid Ibn Badis, as a commentator on the Qur'an, is largely pedagogical and educative. The aim of the author is the general reform of Muslim life, in particular in Algeria, on the basis of a sensible

Islamic doctrine that is recovered in its more authentic meaning. The Qur'an is the point of unavoidable departure; it is the constant meditation on the Qur'an that can bring out the eternal relevance of its message. Ibn Badis defends Qur'anic science and all the traditional religious sciences as the fundamental discipline of Islam, including commentary (*tafsir*), the science of *hadith*, and the acts and sayings of the Prophet that make up the *sunna*, which are all profoundly interconnected. The Qur'anic texts are clear if we take them together, and the traditions of the Prophet are complementary to the Book. As with the Salafiyya, Ibn Badis recommends a return to the sources, in an innovative and not supine way, and the exaltation of the Unity of God (*tawhid*, as emphasized also by 'Abduh) is a foundation bearing the whole of the structure of Islam, and the struggle against superstition of popular mystics, the Marabouts, that offended the purity and the "rational" severity of Islam. The aims of the Qur'an can be identified as the following: (a) to express simply the elements of dogma, (b) to determine the essential rules of what is legal and illegal, a central aspect of a culture like that of Islam, a culture of Law, (c) to put in relief a moral set of values, (d) to draw attention to the wonders of the universe, (e) to encourage "reflective" humanity to notice the signs of God, to consider and understand through reason the design of creation, and (f) to teach the *sunna* and the example of the Prophet.

As we have seen, there are many general indications in the Qur'an that identify it as a book of reference for practical action. This emerges with evidence about political problems that are relatively deep in the work of Ibn Badis. The author recognizes that the Qur'an is a codex of social and political life, but it does not enter into the particular details of how to operate on the level of the effective organization of the state. Authority has a "prophetic" origin and has the ability to defend and apply the law, to spread and preach the good, if necessary with force. Justice is the basis of authority. Commenting on verse 27.21, which deals with Solomon, Ibn Badis writes: "[N]otwithstanding the extension of his power and the majesty of his authority, Solomon was obliged to submit to another and more majestic power than his. This was the power of Right, since the Right is above everyone. Rule has to be based on justice and Solomon accepted the need for respecting the balance of justice. Justice is really the foundation of authority and the bastion of civilization" (quoted in Merad 1971: 207).

This deals with a classical theme of Islamic theology, from al-Ghazali to Ibn Taymiyya to Ibn Khaldun. The other side of the issue is solidarity, a theme that has also been dealt with often by thinkers who, like the Muslim Brothers, find their roots in the Salafiyya, such as Sayyid Qutb and Mustafa al-Siba'i.

The Qur'anic commentary of the Salafiyya is undoubtedly based on a historical point of view, in the sense that it constitutes a response to a particular period and place. The period is one in which the Muslim countries were subject to the dominion of colonial powers and confronted the necessity of rediscovering the roots of Islam in order to resist Western culture founded on science and technology. There was the need for a new kind of commentary, but one that did not go much farther than the traditional commentary. The response to rationality is quite specific and qualified, however. The Qur'an is an open text, inflexible, but open to a modernizing interpretation, and open to a modernizing interpretation because it is itself modern. Some of 'Abduh's legal opinions caused a scandal. Interpreting 4.3, for example, the Egyptian shaykh expressed a lot of doubts on the topic of polygamy. Therefore, he argued, the text could be interpreted and made concrete in a variety of ways.

SPECIFIC TENDENCIES OF *TAFSIR* IN THE TWENTIETH CENTURY: THE LITERARY ASPECTS

The commentary of 'Abduh and Rida brings out the intention to present Islam and its sacred book as sources of knowledge that are completely valid and have nothing to fear from European scientific method and research. A little later, approximately by the middle of the twentieth century, the Qur'anic commentary came to assume a less polemical and militant character, and it returned to a more traditional enquiry consonant with the specific character of Arabic and Muslim culture. The period of traumatic confrontation with the West had ended. From a certain point of view, modernity was something that had to be acquired and could not be eliminated. Politically, the Arab/Islamic world lived through a phase of waiting (the revival took place only after the Second World War with pan-Arabism and socialism, but the political and military struggle with the West took place from the sixties onward). In this phase of waiting, the general approach was for Islamic researchers to present a

Qur'anic interpretation stressing the intrinsic value of the text. The Qur'anic commentators of the first part of the last century might be seen as merely repetitive given the sort of enquiry that took place in the past, such as that of al-Tabari or al-Zamakhshari, for example. It is true that the authors of this period considered themselves mainly participants in a traditional and not particularly original form of research. However, their work did succeed in bringing out what in the Qur'an might be considered relevant for a constructive approach to actual historical reality.

The Egyptians Muhammad Ahmad Khalafallah (1916–1998) and 'A'isha 'Abd al-Rahman Bint al-Shati' (d. 1999) worked particularly between the forties and the sixties. Their commentaries concentrate on the literary quality of the Qur'anic text, in order to show, inevitably, its inimitability, as a feature of its structure. Their leader and shaykh was Amin al-Khuli who, although not having written a Qur'anic commentary himself, showed the way for a new semantic and rhetorical exegesis that had the purpose of detailing the thematic, epistemological and linguistic specificity of the text.

The work of Khalafallah significantly had the title "The Art of Narration in the Qur'an", and it is centered on the analyses of rhetorical and artistic value in most of the stories, parables and narratives contained in the sacred Book. This seems, in summary, to underline the following points:

1. The narrative has as its point bringing out the value of religious truth. This religious truth requires a certain comprehension that is based on the literary analysis of narratives.
2. The events and personalities of the Qur'anic stories are elements that are only to a degree historical and very much simply evocative of what is already known.
3. This material existed generally in Arabia, and the Qur'an used it for religious purposes and not to make a historical point. The purpose is to exhort us to pursue the good and to encourage the development of learning through the narratives (Benzine 2003).

So on this approach, religious truth explains itself in the light of a textual investigation that provides room predominantly for an aesthetic dimension and at the same time a gnomic and directed use of

language. On the other, the aim followed by the Book is not historical but rather is in terms of moral exhortation. All this is not a matter
of chance. A recent critic of Khalafallah, Rachid Benzine, has argued
that the Egyptian exegete wished to point out some pedagogical
aspects of the divine strategy of revelation. This would justify also the
apparent contradictions, imprecisions and incongruences of the text.
The pedagogical meaning does not imply necessarily its philological
and historical accuracy. God used the authority of the imaginary (the
individual in general is easily moved and motivated by wonderful and
edifying stories) in order to make humanity understand. He knew
what to provide in terms of language in general and for the sort of
literature that would appeal to the different kinds of people that exist.
The Qur'anic stories are allegories and do not have to be taken as
literal accounts of authentic historical facts.

It appears that Khalafallah had insisted on the linguistic approach
to interpretation, studying the peculiar composition of stories and
the Qur'anic text. To give just one example, he underlines that the
Qur'an, in describing the final Judgment (in a way that is quite ter-
rifying, as we have seen, especially during the Meccan period), uses
not the perfect case of the verb (that indicates a finished action) but
the imperfect (used in Arabic for the present and also for the future),
and this in the context of producing in the Meccans the fear of
the arrival of the hour that is coming and that convinces them of
their religious fate and moral adequacy, if they abandon their former perverted customs. The use of terms and words is based on a
refined psychology, which is capable of subduing the emotions. In
this perspective, essentially practical, the study of the literary value of
the text is indispensable. It is argued that, to stress the emotive and
psychological value of the text, Khalafallah did not remain faithful
to traditional literalism and wished to introduce meanings that are
other than they seem to be. This is certainly true, but his linguistic/
literary investigation remains focused, it seems to me, on the superficial features of enquiry as the main object of attention so that it can
avoid coming into contact with the problem of historicity. His is a
literary approach, not a hermeneutic method (in the philosophical
sense of the term).

'A'isha Bint al-Shati', the main modern female commentator,
has concentrated on the analyses of the Meccan suras of the Qur'an
(the first suras to be revealed) and has demonstrated a very advanced

philological competence. Her declared intention was that of taking the Qur'an into the sphere of literary and artistic studies and so making it more accessible. Her attention is concentrated for example on the oaths, rather mysterious and allusive, that appear in some of the Meccan chapters, and she has not disregarded in her study the "occasions of revelation" (*asbab al-nuzul*). She wrote: "I set out tentatively to study some brief suras with a definite single argument that among other things date from the first Meccan period, when the Qur'an molded the principles of the 'call' (*da'wa*) of Islam as a faith. I tried to bring out the difference between the usual method of interpreting the Qur'an and ours, which is new, that concerns itself with the Qur'anic text . . . according to the famous old rule through which the sacred Book reveals itself. . . . The specialists in all the schools of Qur'anic studies are in agreement that we have to, first of all, understand the text of the Book. . . . In this way, let us free our interpretation of all extraneous elements and of all defect that is introduced into the nobility of its eloquence" ('A'isha Bint al-Shati' 2004: vol. I: 9–18). Notwithstanding this profession of intent, the method of 'A'isha Bint al-Shati' is not historical. It is a matter of selecting the circumstances that make the Qur'an an autonomous revelation, and the author is also preoccupied with studying the evolution of the meaning of terms inside the text, according to the rhythm and the scansion of revelation. Despite this, she does not really bring into discussion the text itself—insofar as the text is explained, it is in terms of its background that determines it, and with the aim of better understanding the style and literary value. In the decades in which this idea (and also that of Khalafallah) was pursued, it came into conflict with the usual hyper-traditionalist approach to the Qur'an, so that these authors were bitterly challenged by their opponents. Khalafallah, for example, was accused of relativizing the text, making the narratives effects of contingent historical, cultural and psychological experiences.

TRENDS IN THE *TAFSIR* IN THE TWENTIETH CENTURY: "SCIENTIFIC" COMMENTARY

An interpretative approach that has been taken to have had a lot of success and many admirers is what is called *tafsir 'ilmi*, or "scientific" commentary. It works by selecting from within the Qur'an the forecast or the explanation and description of modern scientific discovery. There was a medieval tradition of this type that was referred to by al-Ghazali, as we have seen, who argued that the Qur'an contains the principles of all the sciences. But the contemporary commentator who has contributed most to give dignity to the "scientific" interpretation is an Egyptian, Tantawi Jawhari (d. 1940). This approach argues explicitly for an agreement between the Qur'an and nature and certainly has the merit of linking the holy text with the great currents of scientific thought (for example, it describes Darwinism as a *mutashabih* theory, in reference to verse 3.7, which was much discussed in Chapter 4 in this volume). However, the "scientific" interpretation produces some baffling results. In order to link the literal details of the Qur'an and make them correspond with modern science, the commentators have not only pushed some unlikely equivalences but really forced it into a version that is unacceptable to the text. For example, a Syrian modernist like al-Kawakabi (1854–1902), whom we have already quoted, wrote:

It has been demonstrated that the universe is composed of ether, but already the Qur'an described the beginning of creation: "From the beginning of the construction of Heaven, there was all smoke" (41.11). It has been shown that reality is conditioned by an incessant movement of change, and the Qur'an says "There is a sign for you [human beings] that We have returned to life the dead Earth" and "everything moves on its orbit" (36.33,40). We confirm that the Earth is distinguished from the solar system, and in the Qur'an it is stated "The heavens and the Earth were once joined together and We separated them" (21.30). We have dealt with the way of capturing the dark, that is to photograph, and already in the Qur'an we read: "Do you not look at the works of the Lord, how long he extends the shadow and if he wishes he can make it still. But We make the sun its guide" (25.45). We have discussed how ships and steam or electrical vehicles work, and the Qur'an, after having remarked on the importance of cattle and the wind says: "We created ships similar to it [the Ark] on which they can sail" (36.42). We demonstrate the existence of the microbe and its functions in causing smallpox and other kinds of illness, and the Qur'an says: "The Lord sent them birds Ababil striking them with stones of hard clay" (105.3–4). This is one of many true verses that refer to the scientific context and laws of nature, and by analogy it is possible to put forward interpretations around a multitude of Qur'anic verses, revealing in the future its hidden meaning.

(quoted in Perès 1977: 24f.)

A follower of Jawhari, Ahmad Hanafi, has suggested, even quite recently in the 1960s, that we can find in the Qur'an anticipations of science—for example, Qur'an 21.33: "And God has created the night and the day, the Sun and the Moon, and they swim along (*yasbahuna*) on their course", which suggests to Ahmad Hanafi a proof of the presence of the Copernican cosmology in the Qur'an. He takes the verb *yasbahuna* not as "swimming" but as "hastening" and says that, just as the "night and day" could not be imagined in the act of "hastening", so it has to mean the Earth and the stars. For him the verse means "the Earth, the stars, the Son and the Moon, they all hasten around their course", which according to Ahmad Hanafi implies modern cosmology.

The scientific commentary is vigorously criticized by some Muslims. From 'Abduh to Amin al-Khuli to Sayyid Qutb, many have raised their voices to denounce the ways in which scientific commentary is not only a forced reading of the Qur'anic text but also a betrayal of the original intention of revelation. Qutb, for example, argues, like Galileo, that the scope of Scripture is not scientific and that to interpret the Qur'an scientifically is to limit and hinder the hermeneutic richness of the content of the text. However, the supporters of a scientific reading of the Qur'an have often demonstrated considerable ingenuity, like al-Kawakibi, for example.

An Indian thinker, Abu'l-Kalam Azad (1888–1958), also has sought to structure in a unique order the verses that describe "scientifically" the production of the universe: "The creation of the heavens and the Earth have taken place due to a first matter suggested in the Qur'an by 'smoke' (41.11). This gaseous mass, produced from the start of time, is indivisible [and it is easy to assimilate it to the original nebulosity of the "big bang"]. It has components that are separate and from which the heavenly bodies originate (21.30). The entire universe is not brought into being all at once, but creation has various successive phases, six exactly (10.3). The planets were completed in two periods (41.12). The Earth similarly was created in two periods (41.9). The start of the planets and the completion of the vegetation took place entirely in two periods, since [in the creation of

Earth] they came about in four periods (41.10). The creation of all organisms is verified by leaving the water (21.30). In addition human beings passed through a series of evolutionary stages (71.14)" (quoted in Baljon 1968: 96).

This suggestion reflects the moderately rationalist inclination of some Indian Qur'anic commentators who, under the influence of the nineteenth-century modernist Sayyid Ahmad Khan, have critically discussed the text. Apart from Azad, we should mention Ghulam Ahmad Parwez (1903–1983). These thinkers defended the idea of a possible dynamic reality of the text. Azad has argued that it is not necessary to narrow the Qur'an in significant ways. Asal 'Ali Ashgar Faidi has expressed ideas consonant with those of Mahmud Taha, distinguishing between a Qur'an that is historicized and normative, and a Qur'an that is universal and ethical in its doctrine. Parwez has boldly indicated how not every word of the prophet Muhammad can be considered "revelation". For example, the many places in the Qur'an in which facts and events are described with respect to the life of the Prophet might really be the thoughts and psychological reactions of Muhammad, not strictly in the sense of being "revelation". This is an attempt to reject entirely the anti-utopian inclination that has been stressed from the beginning of this book and can open fertile space for interpretative analysis.

It is worth describing, in the words of Baljon, how Parwez has supported the idea of the rational character with which the Islamic Community came about: "Only a poor bit of belief in the unseen is left over when Parwez—dealing with the problem how to bring the Koranic demand of belief in the unseen into harmony with the Koranic premise of belief's rationality (Q.12.108), 'ala basiratin)—states that for the enforcement of the Koran's social system firstly human faith 'without having seen' is needed, simply because, if its feasibility is to be proved, it has to be put into practice first. Such faith is called iman bi'l-gha'ib [faith in the invisible]. Since results did appear after its coming into operation, belief in the truth of this system will be required" (Baljon 1968: 25). It is a matter then of a position agreeing with the Salafis for whom there is no mystery or secrecy in the Islamic revelation. A preliminary attitude of faith is necessary to approach religion, but then religion contains all the elements required to fulfill its potential and its subsequent rational foundations.

More recently an Algerian physicist, Nidhal Guessoum, discussed thoroughly, from the point of view of a believer philosopher of science, a number of burning questions: evolution, the "intelligent design", quantum mechanics and so on (Guessoum 2011). He approves of Averroes's idea of a harmony between science and religion, because the Qur'an supports the predictability of the world's physical phenomena. It is possible to apply a hermeneutical method to the Qur'an without offending its sacredness. Reconciling Muslim tradition and modern science, however, has yet to face the resistance of traditional literalists because it implies a metaphorical or allegorical reading of the text.

QUR'ANIC EXEGETES: ISLAMIC RADICALS

The fundamental problems that have emerged in introducing this chapter are at the center of reflection on the Qur'an from the perspective of Islamic radicalism. These are issues pertaining to the concept of secularism, which involves the contrast between the modern Islamic state and the political, and envisages a contradiction between religion and civil social life. Islamic radicalism is that current that the mass media define freely as integralist or fundamentalist, that was born in the Arab-Islamic world between the First and Second World Wars, and that, from 1970, radicalized until assuming sometimes "terrorist" forms. Originally, radical or fundamental Islamism denounced contemporary society as corrupt and Godless, affirmed the necessity of a rigorous application of the legislative principles contained in the Qur'an but especially the *sunna*, and in particular defended the necessity of creating an Islamic state that can rule in accordance with principles that are in fact rather nebulous, that of the "sovereignty of God" (*hakimiyya*). The two countries that have seen the birth of political Islamism are Egypt (where in 1928 the Muslim Brothers organization started) and India, then Pakistan (where in 1941 the Jamaat-i Islami got underway), and highly influential thinkers for both movements were Sayyid Qutb (Egyptian) and al-Mawdudi (Pakistani), whom we have already mentioned.

The experience of Qutb is particularly dramatic: imprisoned by Nasser in 1954 and put in prison almost without interruption until his hanging in 1966, as a result of frequent and violent purges by the Egyptian president against the Muslim Brothers. The experience of incarceration and his conviction that the secularism of Nasser went against Islamic tradition had a profound impact on the consciousness of Qutb and has conditioned his vision of reality. His Qur'anic commentary, *In the Shade of the Qur'an* (*Fil Zilal al-Qur'an*), was composed in prison and in addition reveals a dramatic tone and a decidedly extremist conception. Qutb himself explained and elaborated some passages of commentary published in part under the title *Signs Indicating the Path* (*Ma'alim fi'l-tariq*). The book, considered by many to be a sort of breviary of Islamic radicalism, is one of the prohibited texts of the Arab world and is almost impossible to find in libraries but has been republished many times and even translated into English.

Qutb presented this work on the surface as a *tafsir*, not traditional, but as Carré has put it: "The Qur'an is not a dialectical language, by philosophers or theologians, [. . .] but an affective existential language (*wijdani*) on the universe, creation and the arrangement of the universe" (Carré 1984: 39 and 60). The Qur'an is not just a simple literary work; it has divine origin. The Qur'an reflects on the nature of humanity and the whole of reality, acting as a lever on the emotions of those who read and believe in it, with a non-technical language, in some ways like philosophy and theology, but adequate to the specific sensibility of the believer. In other words, the Qur'an has to talk about the "constitution" of the Islamic Community to fit all points of view. There was a golden age of Muhammad and the caliphs who were well guided. We should try to bring back such a state of affairs.

The first generation of Muslims found in the Qur'an all the principles to regulate life. It presented an account of an anti-utopian message: "[T]he first Islamic generations realized truth and justice on earth, and instituted for humanity as a whole an inimitable civilization that has erected its structure, at one time, in the material and spiritual world" (Qutb 1999: vol. I: xii). The turning point in civilization took place as soon as the revelation came down to the Prophet. We have already seen that according to Qutb the Meccan Qur'an has presented a true revolution, in consciousness and in practice. The kernel of the Meccan Qur'an is in fact theocentrism from which social justice may be derived: "The nature of this religion is to be established on the principle of divine Unity. [. . .] [The first Muslims] knew that the formula 'there is no god except God' constitutes a revolution against the worldly power that usurps one of the specific characteristics of divinity [that of making laws]. [. . .] When society is purified of evil, it is brought under the Islamic order, where justice is the justice of God, and balance is the balance of God. The flag of social justice is brought under the name of God alone, and it becomes the flag of Islam" (Qutb 1983: 36, 26, 34).

The theme of social justice is a constant feature of the thought of Qutb, who has dedicated a book to it (which we quoted in the first chapter in this volume). In this last book, as in the Qur'anic commentary, the Unity of God is the guarantee of equality for all of humanity. To profess the Unity of God means to realize the nature of social justice on which the whole Islamic organization rests.

This aim cannot be pursued, according to Qutb, only with prayer and contemplation. The Qur'an reveals its secrets and its treasures only to those who transform their consciousness through action. H'mida Ennaifer quotes a passage in which evidence emerges that suggests making the Qur'an an instrument of *jihad*, of struggle in the way of God: "This Qur'an does not reveal its secrets to those who do not engage in battle and fight a great *jihad*. It is only for those who live in an atmosphere similar to that in which the Qur'an was revealed, someone who experienced and understood it, even though he is not one of those who were addressed by it directly. Such was the first Muslim community, it appreciated and understood the Qur'an and with it became energized" (Ennaifer 1998: 57–58). The presupposition of this methodological position is that Islam is essentially a "movement". In the commentary of Qutb in particular, the "Signs on the way" returns to this idea: "God wished to build society and revolutionary action with doctrine ('*aqida*). He wished to construct doctrine with society and revolutionary action. He wanted the doctrine to establish a social deed and a factual movement. The social deed is found in factual movement and the pure form of doctrine" (Qutb 1983: 45). The dogma of Islam is intertwined with revolutionary movement and a social base.

The approach to the Qur'an is thus an active approach. Commentary itself is essentially a practical engagement. The presuppositions of the study of the Qur'an remain, according to Qutb, a vehicle for one type of meaning—a plurality of interpretations is not possible. This is determined by the practical character of commentary, from the fact that there is a coherence between the Qur'an and the universe. The Qur'an, the authentic word of God, is the Truth, a reflection of the organization of the universe. Truth, Qutb says, is universal: "[A] characteristic of the divine and universal order is that it results inherently in the construction of a universal truth (*haqq*) and that it is not just chance or coincidence. In fact, God himself is the *haqq*" (Qutb 1999: vol. I: xxi). Everything is in its place according to organization and providence. "In the shadow of God" has learned that in existence there is no room for blind coincidence or haphazard events". "We created everything according to a just measure" (54.49). "God is the one who has created everything and has given it its appropriate measure" (25.2). "Everything happens according to a plan, the authentic and deep wisdom that underlies all our existence cannot appear visible to the limited mind of man" (Qutb 1999: vol. I: xix). The Qur'an constitutes the fulcrum of Islam, not only because it reveals the word and will of God, but because it represents the pillar on which Islam operates as a total ideology that is dynamic, realistic and above all balanced.

Al-Mawdudi, together with Qutb the grand theoretician of radicalism, composed a long Qur'anic commentary, originally in Urdu, with the title *Tafhim al-Qur'an*, or "comprehension" of the Qur'an. In fact, the authors draw near to the Qur'an with the necessary humility to comprehend it as a whole, because nowadays many Muslims have lost contact with and comprehension of their sacred book. In the conception of Mawdudi a vision that is distinctly "patriarchal" defines God as the lord or master of the universe and of all creatures, including human beings. People ought not to think of themselves as independent while only God is worthy of obedience, service and adoration.

Rather differently from many of the other Qur'anic commentators, al-Mawdudi does not apparently pay much attention to linguistic or grammatical questions or reflect on the form and style of the Book. His conviction is that the Qur'an is an absolutely "unique" text in theme, content and structure. In a sense it should not be taken as a literary work in the normal meaning of the term. An aspect that stupefied the readers of the Qur'an is its apparent lack of disorganization, so al-Mawdudi comes to argue that the Qur'an follows a marvelous principle of organization. The different parts of the Qur'an are said to have been revealed passage by passage in accord with the whole, with changing needs and the demands of the Islamic movement during the first phases of its birth, its development and its eventual institutionalization. It is then not possible to determine its coherence and systematic consequentialism as though it was a dissertation for a doctorate. The Qur'an is a synthesis and educative amalgam appropriate for diverse times and places, and such a mixture of teachings formulated in different periods provides Islam with an integrated perspective and a complex vision, apart from acting as a safeguard against all deviation and partiality. In any case, the actual arrangement of the Qur'an is not the result of work by earlier writers but was given directly to the Prophet Muhammad on the precise instructions of God. We can observe a sort of providence in the structure of the Qur'an that has its aim at demonstrating its inimitability and the coherence of Islam as a system of thought.

Al-Mawdudi argues that "the mission of each prophet is to invite men to follow the right path, to communicate the genuine instructions of God and to organize in a community everyone who responds to the mission. Such a community ought to dedicate itself to both comprise a model of the right way according to the instructions of God and also to struggle for the reform of the world. The Qur'an is the book that sets out this mission and this guide, according to revelation given to Muhammad" (this and the following passages in al-Mawdudi 1998: vol. I: 7–31 passim). There emerges in this passage two features of Islam from the radical Islamic point of view. The doctrine is essentially praxis, practical action in order to further the realization of a new moral, social and political order. "The Qur'an is not a book of abstract theory or cold doctrine that the reader can grasp while sitting comfortably in his armchair nor is it merely a religious book like other religious books, in which the secrets are hidden and have to be revealed in seminaries and oratories. The Qur'an is on the contrary the program and the blueprint of a message, of a mission and so of a movement". Al-Mawdudi does not think that the Qur'an represents an integral legislative code since "to put it briefly, the Book contains general and non-specific principles, that provide details of minute legal matters. The scope of the Book is to explain in a clear and appropriate manner the intellectual and moral bases of the Islamic program for life. Its method of guidance for practical life does not consist in setting out specific laws and regulations. It prefers to trace a guideline by which people can organize themselves in accordance with the will of God. The mission of the Prophet is to confer practical form on the Islamic vision of existence offering to the world a model of individual character and, at a particular time, of the state and human society, living incarnations of the principles of the Qur'an". We can see how for al-Mawdudi, as for those who have similar views from a traditional perspective, the correct Islamic doctrine ought to base itself on the Qur'an, in the first place, but also it is the case that the Qur'an ought to become integrated with the *sunna* of the Prophet.

Notwithstanding this profession of intent, al-Mawdudi, following the details in his commentary, does not make much use of the hadith, as an exemplar of what passes as the norm in commentary according to authority and tradition. The investigation follows a line that is very clear and where the exposition is plain and far from technical, in order to encourage general understanding. Another singular aspect is that, notwithstanding the author having argued with clarity that the Qur'an is a Book that ought to guide all action and all political endeavor, he rarely gets involved in political analysis (very different from the case of Qutb). A noteworthy exception is the commentary on sura 17, in which al-Mawdudi claims that the assumption of political power is necessary in Islam in order to realize reform. It is a mistake to argue that issues dealing with power and the state are merely "wordly". As we have seen, the commentary of Qutb is decidedly practical, while that of al-Mawdudi is more educative and didactic, rather similar to the Salafi commentators.

THE HISTORICITY OF THE TEXT

As we have seen, in the interpretive analyses of radical Islamism, the tendency prevails to argue that the text contains just one kind of meaning, while some contemporary commentators have produced evidence of the necessity to pursue a historical approach that inevitably contextualizes and pluralizes the meaning of the text. All these commentators are thinkers (and often philosophers) who are preoccupied with renewing Islam in a manner that we might define as "secular" and as far removed from the point of view of both traditional approaches to commentary as well as to the radicals.

Among the personalities that are particularly worth noting is the Algerian (subsequently French and a professor at the Sorbonne) Muhammad Arkoun (1928–2010). His studies on the Qur'an are

not systematic and take more of the form of a suggestive and speculative methodology that can be applied to the study of the text. Being
a philosopher, Arkoun has explored the possibility of a specifically
philosophical hermeneutics that would bring out the resources of
scientific humanism (the account that follows is based on two of
his essays, "Bilan et perspectives des études coraniques" and "Comment lire le Koran?", both contained in Arkoun 1982: v–xxxiii and
1–26). He is interested in distinguishing in the structure of a culture
and a mentality between the "thinkable", the "unthinkable" and
the "unthought". The "thinkable" is "that which it is possible to
think and explain, with the help of the conceptual scheme, from the
point of view of a linguistic community in a given period". Right
away in this definition emerges the great importance that Arkoun
gives to linguistic factors, especially those linked with a historical
period. If this is the thinkable, the unthought is apparently what
lies far beyond the boundaries of the existing intellectual/linguistic
schema. In terms of this the unthought becomes the unthinkable.
A culture or a civilization defends the thinkable as the only possible form of expression and, distinguishing it sharply from what is
unthought, makes unthinkable whatever a particular culture or civilization refuses to think about.

According to Arkoun, historicity represents a fundamental
"unthought" factor of Islam. This is due to the fact that "the Discourse [the author means the sacred texts and in particular the Qur'an]
becomes the official corpus and generator of transcendence". In the
traditional commentaries, the Qur'an contains everything that can be
thought, and the traditional commentators claim that through their
study of the Qur'an they have mapped out and expressed everything
that can be thought. But there is a need to open up the unthought
and make of it something that becomes thinkable: "[T]he accom-
plishment of Islamic thought is to renounce apologetic discourses, all
anaesthetizing of the spirits to take up its right role in the struggle in
the course of conquering meaning, through a better control of the
destiny of man in each society and in the general movement of history". As a result the Qur'an has developed a "false consciousness"
that ought to be denounced and opposed, as thinkers like Nietzsche,
Marx and Freud have denounced and destroyed the "false consciousness" of Western culture. Taking the Qur'an to be everything that

is thinkable turns modernity into the unthought, and the supporters of traditionalism can then regard modernity as unthinkable. Arkoun proposes to support a historical reading "that does not separate man from transcendence, but obliges him to follow transcendence in the historical reality in which it is incarnated in many different ways". Transcendence then is not annulled or negated by the application of the Qur'an as a historical project. On the contrary, it comes to be seen in terms of how far it is significant in different historical circumstances.

An essential hermeneutic presupposition produced by the author is that "we need to consider the text in its totality in a system of internal *relations*". This is because it becomes essential to discover the *structural* order of the text. To this end, Arkoun suggests a series of methods from the human sciences—first, linguistics and semiotics (Arkoun has a high regard for Khalafallah), and then social criticism and historical psychology. Language, society and history are three approaches to making a definite reading in three ways. There is "a) a linguistic way that allows us to discover a profound order in an apparent disorder, b) an anthropological way that would consist in recognizing the role of language as a mythical structure [what we have called "anti-utopianism" Arkoun defines as "return to mythical consciousness"] and c) an historical way which defines the possibilities and the limits of logical/lexicographical exegeses and imaginative exegeses that are produced up to now by Muslims". Like all contemporary Muslims, Arkoun has energetically sought to renew the importance and the role of the Qur'an in Islamic society. "The study of the Qur'an and Islamic thought in the way in which we have defined it has to respond to three urgent needs: a) to overcome once and for all the ethnocentric mentality and theological exclusivity, b) to develop a scientific approach in which Revelation, Truth and History are considered in their dialectical relations with defining terms of human existence, c) to reassemble contemporary consciousness and the languages in which they are expressed". It is evident that these professions of intent have to have a decisive social impact. But Arkoun limits himself to following a cultural and philosophical end, underlining how work on the Qur'an can make it become an instrument "for the elaboration of a humanism in the light of our times".

THE HUMANISTIC HERMENEUTICS
OF NASR ABU ZAYD

The thesis of Arkoun has had a big impact. Its author has been vehemently criticized by engaged Muslim thinkers like Muhammad Talbi who charged him not to be a true Muslim, but he has not been anathematized (perhaps because he lived in France). Nasr Hamid Abu Zayd has been a contemporary Egyptian thinker (1943–2010) whose theoretical work on the Qur'an has led to bitter and heated debates that have resulted in his marginalization in Egypt and finally forced him to immigrate to the Netherlands. The thesis of Abu Zayd appears provocative from the traditional Islamic perspective, and that is not so much because he sought to define the contours of a hermeneutic enquiry as because he saw that hermeneutics as being very much part of the "concept of the text" and of its decisive historicization. Abu Zayd sets out to argue for the historicity of the text and its language. It is enough here to produce some quotations: "The text is a cultural and historical product" (Abu Zayd 1999: 27). Such a perspective has a series of important implications. The first is that, returning to theology, the doctrine of the Mu'tazilites that the Qur'an was created appears to be more modern and scientific than the Ash'arite view, and it frees the potentiality of the text. The uncreated text of the Ash'arites is the Qur'an in which the work of God is definitely delivered, and that produce interpretations that only go in one direction. The created Qur'an tends to support the possibility of a rational reading, leaving behind fundamental dogma. On the other hand, Abu Zayd argued that "religious texts are in the last analysis nothing but linguistic texts, in the sense that they belong to a determined cultural structure, that they have been produced in conformity to the laws that govern the culture in which they have started and whose language is, rightly, the principal semiotic system" (Abu Zayd 1999: 63). Now, the linguistic signs change the literary contents of a text in symbols, and "the linguistic analysis is the only means offered to everyone to understand the Qur'anic message and apart from that, Islam itself" (Abu Zayd 1999: 32). What can be protected is then not the literal meaning but the symbol. The symbol acts as the banner and point of reference for all those who interpret the Book and forms the basis of action that is appropriate for all social and historical reality.

From the perspective of Abu Zayd, the text lives through its connection with the activity of people: "Reality is the basis that cannot be hidden. And this reality can come out of the text from a determined and specific culture and language. Through its contact with the actions of people the sense of the text is renewed" (Abu Zayd 1999: 188). An event initiated by revelation, the Qur'an entered into history. If this sounds rather secular, it is because its transcendent cause (God) made it an instrument for dealing with people who live in the world. Secularism does not imply a reification of the text; it does not become something else with respect to the intentions of its author (God). However, the reduction of the text to the level of human reason and the human capacity to act frees the power of meaning and also of interpretation: "The Qur'an is a religious text definitely fixed from the point of view of literal meaning, but when it is subject to human reason, it becomes the 'Concept' that loses its fixity while its meanings proliferate" (Abu Zayd 1992: 93).

In fact Abu Zayd refuted the classical traditional commentary of Tabari or Zamakhshari in favor of a philosophical interpretation that is not a mere analysis of the text but implies the inescapability of the hermeneutic circle between the interpreter and the interpreted. On the one hand interpreters apply themselves to the text and analyze it in the light of their "prejudices" (the terminology and the concepts are Gadamer's). On the other the text preserves its objective and literal value. In this way, the hermeneutist suggests a return to the original roots of the text, and also the prospect of seeking the aim and context of the text. Seeking the aim of the text, according to the intentions of the observer, is not to make it rigid conceptually and predetermined ideologically, but it opens up a great multiplicity of interpretations. The Qur'an, as al-Ghazali put it, becomes a "deep sea" of symbols and precious stones, since the possible meanings of the text are infinite. This perspective is clearly expressed by Ennaifer: "What Abu Zayd proposed in his hermeneutic reading is to consider that the interruption in revelation with the death of the Prophet did not change the nature of the relations between the text and reality. This relationship follows in a dialectical manner with our comprehension of the text becoming enlarged and changes in accordance with the facts of reality. And this is what Abu Zayd called hermeneutic pluralism. In a word, he thought that the text has an independent existence and the reader his own horizon. Thanks to its structure, science and its exegetical and interpretative estate has a relationship with the mind of the reader. The reader is able to lead the text to its horizon" (Ennaifer 1998: 96). The delicate problem is that, from the point of view of traditional Islam, asking about the historicity and the secularization of the text is to put its sacred nature in danger. Abu Zayd has been accused of apostasy, but his ideas cannot properly be described in that way; rather they confirm, from the point of views of both faith and intellect, the profound Ghazalian convictions that the Qur'an can be considered the epitome of knowledge of morality and justice. The important thing is to preserve the symbolic sense of the text. Its sacred nature is guaranteed by the purity of its source.

It is worth pointing out that after his earlier controversial views Abu Zayd has taken a different direction in his thought and interpretation. Unfortunately, he has not described systematically his ideas in a published book that would have set out his new approach because of his untimely death. The point of departure was a real turn around, since the Qur'an is not considered so much a text (*nass*) but rather a discourse, or, better, a system of discourses. The approach is to completely overturn the fact. The Qur'an as a text can have a determinate structure (*tartib*), a structure that is fixed, to its physical form, to the fact of containing 114 chapters collected in a precise order, a number of verses that are Meccan and Medinan, phrases and words that cannot change their context and meaning, and so on. In this sense, the Qur'an is what the Muslims call the *mushaf*, or "the book" in its proper meaning, a manuscript or printed document on pages that are brought together with a book cover. The *mushaf* is different in dogmatic, historical and spiritual content that comes to represent what really is the "Qur'an". The fact of confusing the *mushaf* with "Qur'an", the exterior and literal aspect with the living aspect of the content, has turned the Qur'an into a closed and silent body, embalmed in its objectivity. The Qur'an as a text obviously has an author, God, who has composed it for specific ends (*maqasid*). Since these ends are predetermined by the divine will, it is not possible in any way to place in discussion its direction or meaning. The concept of the Qur'an as a text makes impossible any dialectic, so the reading of the Qur'an becomes an obligatory reading, and almost metaphysical, and the text is turned into a dogma. This is the reason why Islamic theology, both Mu'tazilite and Ash'arite, considered the meaning of the Qur'an as fixed in the *mushaf*. This idea is based on a vertical agreement between humanity and God through revelation, while at the end of his life Abu Zayd defended the idea of a horizontal agreement, of a continuous dialogue between God and humans, which serves to put the interlocutors on a level of communication with nothing imposed. The Qur'an serves as we saw at the beginning to bring God in contact with humanity, but, while with the conception of the Qur'an as text the two interlocutors occupy a position that differ spatially, now with the conception of the Qur'an as a system of discourses the position is basically more favorable to humans, since humanity is then free to interpret.

Seen in this way, the Qur'an has a structure that is open to a number of parallel interpretations. Also, the Qur'an does not have just one or even more than one meaning or determinate end, as is often suggested in the case of the concept of a text. The Qur'an presents different options according to different situations in which it was revealed. However, in some sense it maintains its historical character. For example, it is possible to find in the Qur'an invitations to war and invitations to peace. From the perspective of Abu Zayd, it means not that the Qur'an is a text totally urging peace or the reverse but that different verses point to peace and to war and they were revealed in response to precise circumstances in history and the prophetic experience of Muhammad and the affirmation of Islam as a religion.

The consequences of such a suggestion are important. In the first place, the Qur'an as a discourse or collection of discourses is essentially a dialogue and debate. It is not the vehicle for just one ideology, immutable and metaphysical, but calls on its readers and hearers to relate to it, to dialectic, to the exchange of opinions. The flexibility of the Qur'an that earlier seemed guaranteed only by interpretations, through hermeneutical activity, seems now guaranteed by the fact that it obliges its readers (and believers) to reflect ethically and morally, to examine theological possibilities, to determine rules about behavior that can respond to life in a diverse way to all the necessities that may arise.

This is not just a simple conceptual revision. Abu Zayd added:

> I recently started to realize how dealing with the Qur'an as solely a text reduces its status and ignores the fact that it is still functioning as a "discourse" in everyday life. The volume entitled "The Qur'an as Text", which presents the proceedings of the symposium held in 1993 in the Oriental Seminar of the University of Bonn, enjoyed so many reprints, because

it introduces the shift to which Stefan Wild refers, at least in Western Qur'anic scholarship, from the paradigm of the "genesis" of the Qur'an, whether Jewish or Christian, to the paradigm of textus receptus.

It is true that the Qur'anic textus receptus, the Qur'an as a text contained in the mushaf, shaped and shapes the religious convictions of Muslims and, moreover, is the central cultural text in so many Islamic cultures. But this is true only when we limit our definition of "convictions" and "cultures" to the high level, the "convictions", and "cultures" of the elite. On the lower level of convictions and cultures, on the level of the masses, it is more the recited Qur'an, the phenomenon of the Qur'an as discourse, that plays the most important role in shaping public consciousness.

For Muslim scholars the Qur'an was always a text, from the moment of its canonization till now. It is time now to pay close attention to the Qur'an as discourse or discourses. It is no longer sufficient to re-contextualize a passage or some passages when it is only necessary fight against literalism and fundamentalism or when it is necessary to renounce a certain historical practice that seems unfit in our modern context. It is also not enough to invoke modern hermeneutics in order to justify the historicity and, therefore, the relativity of every mode of understanding claiming in the meantime that our modern interpretation is the more appropriate and the more valid. These insufficient approaches produce either polemic or apologetic hermeneutics.

Without rethinking the Qur'an, without re-invoking its living status as a "discourse", whether in the academia or in everyday life no democratic and open hermeneutics can be achieved. But why should hermeneutics be democratic and open? Because it is about the "meaning of life". If we are serious about freeing religious thought from power manipulation, whether political, social, or religious in order to empower the community of believers to formulate "meaning", we need to construct open democratic hermeneutics.

(Abu Zayd 2004: 27–28)

THE NEW HERMENEUTICS OF FAZLUR RAHMAN

A perspective that ought to be discussed in the hermeneutic line is also that of one of the outstanding thinkers of the twentieth century, Fazlur Rahman (1919–1988). He was persecuted in his own country (Pakistan) because of accusations that he had produced very audacious ideas, and Rahman (1982: 8–9) sought to read Islam as a conception of the world projected on the modern. Relative to the Qur'an, he began by criticizing "the 'atomistic' approach of many interpreters who failed to understand the underlying unity of the Qur'an, coupled with a practical insistence upon fixing on the words of various verses in isolation". Rahman criticized at the same time the philosophers and the mystics: "The philosophers and often the Sufis did understand the Qur'an as a unity, but this unity was imposed upon the Qur'an (and Islam in general) from without rather than derived from a study of the Qur'an itself".

The need to study the Qur'an as a unity, as a structure, lead Rahman to elaborate a method in two phases. The first consists of deriving from the historical reality of the Qur'an the general universal valid principles, from a theological and moral point of view, for humanity. The second consists in the application of the subsequent principles on the level of praxis:

> The process of interpretation proposed here consists of a double move-ment, from the present situation to Qur'anic times, then back to the present. The Qur'an is the divine response, through the Prophet's mind, to the moral-social situation of the Prophet's Arabia. [. . .] The Qur'an and the genesis of the Islamic community occurred in the light of history and against a social-historical background. The Qur'an is a response to that situation. [. . .] The first of the two movements mentioned above consists of two steps. . . . The first step of the first movement consists of understand-ing the meaning of the Qur'an as a whole as well as in terms of the specific tenets that constitute responses to specific situations. The second step is to generalize those specific answers and enunciate them as statements of general moral-social objectives that can be "distilled" from specific texts in the light of socio-historical background and the often-stated rationes legis. [. . .] Whereas the first movement has been from the specifics of the Qur'an to the eliciting and systematizing of its general principles, values and long-range objectives, the second is to be from this general view to the specific view that is to be formulated and realized now. That is, the general has to be embodied in the present concrete socio-historical context.
>
> (Rahman 1982: 5–6)

The context of ideas, argued Rahman, is not exclusively mental but also contextual. That implies a strong critique of the hermeneutic approach of Hans Gadamer: "Gadamer maintains his phenomeno-logical doctrine according to which all experience of understanding presupposes a preconditioning of the experiencing subject and there-fore, without due acknowledgment of this fact of being predetermined (which is the essence of Gadamer's entire hermeneutical theory), any attempt to understand anything is doomed to unscientific vitia-tion. What so predetermines me as an understanding subject is what Gadamer calls 'the effective history', that is not only the historical influence of the object of investigation, but the totality of other influ-ences that make up the very texture of my being. Thus there is no question of any 'objective understanding of anything at all' " (Rahman 1982: 8–9). According to Rahman, Gadamer establishes the objectiv-ity of the text by providing an excess of suggested conditions that enter the issue in a prejudicial way before it is entirely understood. It does mean that the subjective prejudices and presuppositions of the reader can condition a factual (objective) approach to the text. On the contrary, in Rahman's view, "in the case of the Qur'an, the objec-tive situation is a necessary condition for understanding, particularly since, in view of its absolute normativity for Muslims, it is literally God's response through Muhammad's mind (this latter factor has been radically underplayed by the Islamic orthodoxy) to a historic situation (a factor likewise drastically restricted by the Islamic orthodoxy in a real understanding of the Qur'an)" (Rahman 1982: 8). The cohesion between the objective situation of the text and the objective situa-tion of the historical context—modernity and contemporaneity—in which the text ought to be applied leads Rahman to an affirmation of the difficulty of reception from the point of view of a traditionalist Muslim on which he comments:

> The contention that certainty belongs not to the meanings of particular verses of the Qur'an and their content (by "certainty" I mean not their revealed char-acter for undoubtedly the Qur'an is revealed in its entirety, but the certainty of our understanding of their true meaning and import) but to the Qur'an as a whole, that is as a set of coherent principles or values where the total teach-ings will converge, might appear shocking to many Muslims.
>
> (Rahman 1982: 4)

Rahman explicitly defends the historicity of the text. He defends as extremely important for the reestablishment of Islamic thought the necessity to destroy the anti-utopian attitude that immobilizes the future in repetition and in the imitation of the past and, as we have seen, risks the reification of the text with respect to the author. The last quotation represents a clear condemnation of the rigidity of interpretation and traditional Islamic theology. The defense of the historicity of the text is possible from a hermeneutic perspective.

HERMENEUTICS FOR LIBERATION: FARID ESACK AND AMINA WADUD

The presupposition of liberation theology is monotheism. As Hasan Hanafi has written, "Theology of Liberation expresses the theology of the Twentieth Century, a century of liberation movements in the Third World where the Muslim lands exist. Monotheism took again the original meaning, the liberation of humanity from all kinds of oppression, whether from nature or from man. The first expression of faith in Islam begins with a negation 'I do not believe in any other deities except the Only God'. Deities change from time to time. They are the wrong ideals for any community. Any overwhelming power is a deity. Colonialism, imperialism, feudalism, capitalism, all overwhelming powers to be rejected as deities of our time" (Hanafi 1977: 127) . On this view the hermeneutics of liberation begins with verse 2.218: "Those who believe, and who move home and struggle in the way of God, they have hope in and mercy from God". The verse naturally reflects the conditions of Muslims who had left Mecca for Medina and in Medina were fighting "on the way of God" against the Meccans. The interpretation of this verse, as Hanafi shows, implies the translation of comprehension into action, into praxis.

South African Farid Esack has argued:

I believe that a Muslim's task of understanding the Qur'an within a context of oppression is twofold. First, it is to expose the way traditional interpretation and beliefs about a text function as ideology in order to legitimize an unjust order. A text dealing with fitna—(literally, "disorder")—would, for example, be critically re-examined in order to see how the word has come to be broadly interpreted as challenges to the dominant political status quo, however unjust that status quo may be. Second, it is to acknowledge the wholeness of the human being, to extract the religious dimensions within that situation of injustice from the text and utilize this for the cause of liberation. (One would, for example, ask questions about the relationship of God to hunger and exploitation). These theological dimensions simultaneously shape and are being shaped by the activity of those Islamists engaged in a struggle for justice and freedom.

[. . .]

My advocacy of a South African Qur'anic hermeneutics of religious pluralism for liberation [is grounded on]:

1. One cannot escape from the personal or social experiences which make up the sum of one's existence. Therefore, any person reading a text or viewing any situation does so through the lenses of his or her experiences.

2. Anyone's attempts to make sense of anything read or experienced take place in a particular context. Because every reader approaches the Qur'an within a particular context, it is impossible to speak of an interpretation of the Qur'anic text applicable to the whole world. Meaning is always tentative and biased.

3. According to the Qur'an, one arrives at correct beliefs (orthodoxy) through correct actions (orthopraxis) (Q. 29, 69). The latter is the criterion by which the former is decided. In a society where injustice and poverty drive people to say "even God has left, no one cares anymore", orthopraxis really means activity which supports justice, i.e., liberative praxis. A Qur'anic hermeneutics of liberation therefore emerges within concrete struggles for justice and derives its authenticity from that engagement.

(Esack 1997: 11–13)

This obviously deals with a hermeneutics of liberation that the circumstances of apartheid have made necessary. The concepts of *jihad* as "striving for improvement of human conditions" and of *taqwà* as "accountability to God" pave the way to the concept of *nas*. *Nas* means "people", and "given the stewardship of humankind on earth and God's overwhelming concern for them", the Qur'an has to be interpreted in support of the interest of people, opposing the oppression of the privileged minorities over the interest of majority (Esack 1997:96).

The "gender *jihad*" grounded upon a revolutionary exegesis of the Qur'an is the method of Amina Wadud's struggle for the liberation of women. An African American, born Christian in 1952 and converted to Islam still in her youth, Wadud claims that "true" Islam is completely different from the prevalent machist interpretation of (male) conservative Muslims. Islam is not in itself to be guilty of the women's subordination in traditional Muslim societies. *Islam* means not "submission" but *engaged surrender* to God's will, involving an active attitude toward life that expresses itself in civil and social commitment for humankind's improvement in obedience with God's laws. God made the human being God's vicegerent or *khalifa* on earth, giving him or her free will and liberty and capacity to act. Both are characteristic of males and females as well, but first of all of women. In this sense, the activist approach to religion and history is a "gender *jihad*" aimed primarily to women's liberation.

Qur'an and Woman, which the author presents as a "gender study", made Amina Wadud famous all over the world (Wadud 1992). She claims the necessity of hermeneutics in the footsteps of Gadamer and Fazlur Rahman. She faces the thorny exegetical issues of contextualization and historicization of the text. For example, using mainly linguistic devices, she tries to demonstrate that the controversial verse 4.34, which apparently sanctions the subordination of women to men, in reality is aimed to suggest that men must be "provident" and "sympathizing" toward their women in a mutual effort of comprehension and support.

Wadud's point of view is characteristically "feminine" or "feminist" indeed, and this is possible because the Qur'an's notion of God transcends the gender differences. In the Qur'an, God is neither male nor female, while in Christianity "It" is decisively male. If something, the Islamic God is "female" insofar as Its most important attributes, *rahman* and *rahim* (the compassionate, the merciful), derive from the same Arab root expressing maternal womb.

CONCLUSION

The evolution of contemporary commentary seems to point to the increasingly diffuse necessity for an open reading of the Qur'an in the sense of social, cultural and political commitment. A mystic said "progressive revelation of the Qur'an is accomplished through the text, but not through its meaning". The conquest of meaning is the challenge that presents itself to Muslims who now reflect on their sacred text. A Dutch scholar, Baljon, has written:

> Every Holy Book is loaded with the ambivalence both of being originated in a given space of time (its "earthly" character) and of pretending to offer transcendent information and everlasting values for the believer of whatever age (its "heavenly" aspect). The ineluctable consequence of this contradictory datum for the interpreter who wants to keep pace with the times, is to engage in apologetics in order to prove that the Holy Scripture adequately meets the needs of the present, both materially and spiritually. Consequently, the transcendent has to be made actual!
>
> (Baljon 1968: 88)

Apologetics is always in the position of looking backward; it blunts the critical resources of the text, limiting it to a defense of already supplied meaning toward the new. The philosophical hermeneutics (the modern version of *ta'wil* as opposed to traditional *tafsir*) can also agree to arrive at the same result, as we have seen in the positions of Arkoun and Abu Zayd. It is certainly a problem if philosophical hermeneutics remains a mere verbal exercise. A contemporary thinker like Hasan Hanafi demonstrates that what Baljon considers paradoxical (the transcendent that becomes actual) is instead a presupposition of the whole enterprise. Hanafi writes that "after the process of understanding comes the problem of realization of the meaning of human life. Praxis is the fulfillment of the Logos. Dogmas do not exist by themselves, but dogma, that signifies an idea or a motivation, is entirely praxis" (Hanafi 1977: 18). This refers to a hermeneutics that can be defined as one of liberation. This possibility is expressed nowadays, as we have seen, by a number of thinkers in very interesting ways.

The hermeneutic meaning of Hanafi's argument is an extension of his more ambitious general project to translate theology into anthropology. He is trying to replace the issue of the essence of God with the vital necessity for humans to insert themselves into history. Theology, the science of God, ought to become the science of humanity and be prepared for a reconquest, from poverty and humility to dignity. This project can perhaps be considered in agreement theoretically with the interpretative work of Abu Zayd. The latter brought together what is behind this attempt of the historicization of

Islam, and their fundamental ideologies have more in common than is usually the case with Islamic thinkers. For instance, both stand in opposition to anti-utopianism. The Qur'an appears to be the first of the doctrinal and ideological foundations of Islam that ought to be supported by such a revision. The resistance to this process continues and is strong in countries where traditionalist Muslim intellectuals see in such revisions a threat introducing secular culture and damaging the stability of Muslim society. The resolution of this problem should take place, and Qur'anic commentary will certainly survive and flourish in its continuing encounter with such a variety of points of view, more and more affirming as instrument of praxis.

SUMMARY

In this chapter we have dealt with

- The crisis of Islam in response to modernity.
- The Salafi commentaries of the Qur'an with particular attention to the Manar commentary by 'Abduh and Rida.
- The linguistic commentaries of Khalafallah and Bint al-Shati'.
- The "scientific commentary" that seeks to identify in the Qur'an the scientific laws of nature.
- The radical commentaries of the "fundamentalist thinkers" Sayyid Qutb and al-Mawdudi.
- The modern hermeneutics of thinkers like Arkoun, Abu Zayd and Rahman who have struggled to develop a historical interpretation of the Holy text.
- The Qur'an as a basis for the Islamic theology of liberation in Farid Esack and Amina Wadud.
- The Qur'anic exegesis as instrument of praxis.

REFERENCES/READINGS

Abduh, M. *Risalat al-tawhid: Exposé de la Religion Musulmane*, Geuthner, Paris 1978.

Abu Zayd, N. *Naqd al-Khitab al-Dini,* Dar al-Thaqafa al-Jadida, Cairo 1992 (French translation by N. Abu Zayd (Abou Zeid), *Critique du Discours Religieux,* Sindbad Actes Sud, cit. 1999).

Abu Zayd, N. *Mafhum al-nass (The Concept of Text),* Markaz al-Thaqafi al-'Arabi, Beirut-Casablanca 2000.

Abu Zayd, N. "Rethinking the Qur'an: Toward a Humanistic Hermeneutics", *Islamochristiana* XXX, 2004, pp. 25–45.

A'isha 'Abd al-Rahman Bint al-Shati, *Al-Tafsir al-Bayani lil'Qur'an al-Karim*, Dar al-Ma'arif, Cairo 2004.

Arkoun, M. *Lectures du Coran*, Maisonneuve, Paris 1982.

Arkoun, M. *The Unthought in Contemporary Islamic Thought*, Al-Saqi and the Institute of Ismaili Studies, London 2002.

Baljon, J.M.S. *Modern Muslim Koran Interpretation (1880–1960)*, Brill, Leiden 1968.

Barlas, A. Amina Wadud's Hermeneutics of the Qur'an: Women rereading Sacred Texts, in S. Taji-Farouki (ed.), *Modern Muslim Intellectuals and the Qur'an*, Oxford University Press and the Institute of Ismaili Studies, London 2004, pp. 97–124.

Benzine, R. comment to Khalafallah, *Al-Fann al-qasasi fi'l-Qur'an*, in www.etudes-musulmanes.com/textes, downloaded February 2003.

Campanini, M. Dall'unicità di Dio alla rivoluzione: un percorso fenomenologico di Hasan Hanafi, negli Atti del Convegno Teologie politiche dei monoteismi, a cura di G. Filoramo, *Rappresentazioni del divino e dinamiche del potere*, Morcelliana, Brescia 2004, pp. 215–230.

Campanini, M. *The Qur'an: Modern Muslim Interpretations*, Routledge, London-New York 2011.

Carré, O. *Mystique et politique: Lecture Révolutionnaire du Coran par Sayyid Qutb*, Cerf, Paris 1984.

Cooper, J., Nettler, R. and Mahmoud, M. (eds.), *Islam and Modernity: Muslim Intellectuals Respond*, I.B. Tauris, London 2000.

Ennaifer, H. *Les Commentaires Coraniques Contemporains: Analyse de leur Méthodologie*, Pontificio Istituto di Studi Arabi e di Islamistica, Roma 1998.

Esack, F. *Qur'an: Liberation and Pluralism*, Oneworld, Oxford 1997.

Guessoum, N. *Islam's Quantum Question: Reconciling Muslim Tradition and Modern Science*, I.B. Tauris, London-New York 2011.

Hanafi, H. Théologie ou Anthropologie?, in Anouar Abdel Malek et al. (eds.), *Renaissance du Monde Arabe*, Duculot, Gembloux 1972, pp. 233–264.

Hanafi, H. *Religious Dialogue and Revolution*, Anglo-Egyptian Bookshop, Cairo 1977.

Jansen, J. *The Interpretation of the Koran in Modern Egypt*, Brill, Leiden 1980.

Jomier, J. *Le Commentaire coranique du Manar*, Maisonneuve, Paris 1954.

al-Kawakibi, Tyranny's Characteristics, Cairo 1900, in H. Perès (ed.), *La Littérature Arabe et l'Islam par les Textes*, Maisonneuve, Paris 1977, pp. 24–28.

Kepel, G. *Jihad: The Trail of Political Islam*, I.B. Tauris, London 2002.

Laroui, A. *Islam et Modernité*, La Découverte, Paris 1986.

al-Mawdudi, *Towards Understanding the Qur'an*, edited by Zafar I. Ansari, The Islamic Foundation, Leicester 1998.

Merad, A. *Ibn Badis Commentateur du Coran*, Geuthner, Paris 1971.

Perès, H. (ed.). *La Littérature Arabe et l'Islam par les Textes*, Maisonneuve, Paris 1977.

Peters, R. *Jihad in Classical and Modern Islam*, Markus Wiener, Princeton 1996.

PISAI (Pontifical Institute for Arabic and Islamic Studies), *Le Commentaire Coranique Contemporain*. Deuxième Partie. Le Tafsir Moderne et Contemporain, Dossier des Etudes Arabes, n. 69, 1985.

Qutb, S. *Ma'alim fi'l-tariq*, Dar al-Shuruq, Cairo-Beirut 1983. English text on the web: www.youngmuslims.ca/online_library/books/milestones and other sites.

Qutb, S. *The Islamic Concept and Its Characteristics*, American Trust Publications, Indianapolis 1991.

Qutb, S. *In the Shade of the Qur'an*, edited by M.A. Salahi and A.A. Shamis, The Islamic Foundation, Leicester 1999.

Rahman, F. *Islam and Modernity*, University of Chicago Press, Chicago 1982.

Rahman, F. *Major Themes of the Qur'an*, Chicago University Press, Chicago 2001.

Ramadan, T. *Aux Sources du Renoveau Musulman: d'al-Afghani à Hasan al-Banna un Siècle de Réformisme Islamique*, Bayard, Paris 1998.

Sivan, E. *Radical Islam: Medieval Theology and Modern Politics*, Yale University Press, New Haven-London 1990.

Taji-Farouki, S. (ed.). *Modern Muslim Intellectuals and the Qur'an*, Oxford University Press and the Institute of Ismaili Studies, Oxford-New York-London 2004.

Wadud, A. *Qur'an and Woman,* Oxford University Press, Oxford-New York 1992.

Watt, W.M. *Islamic Fundamentalism and Modernity*, Routledge, London-New York 1988.

Watt, W.M. *Muslim-Christian Encounters*, Routledge, London 1991.

APPENDIX I

GLOSSARY OF ESSENTIAL TERMS

Ahl al-kitab   "People of the Book" or "of Scripture", the people for whom a "book" has been revealed containing the declaration of monotheism, especially the Jews, Christians and Zoroastrians.

Amr   "Order" of God, often linked with *ruh* (spirit) but sometimes also with *khalq* (creation). Indicates the rules and decisions of God with reference to revelation as well as to the construction of the world.

ʿAql   "Intellect" or "intelligence". The Qurʾan exhorts everywhere humans to use their intelligence to understand creation and reflect on God's signs.

Asbab al-nuzul   "Circumstances" or "occasions" of revelation, meaning the contingent events and historical facts that have determined the "coming down" of revelation.

al-Asmaʾ al-Husnà   The "beautiful names of God". According to tradition there are ninety-nine, while a hundredth secret name exists only known to God.

Aya   Literally "sign", meaning both a single Qurʾanic verse and the entire Qurʾan itself as a "sign" of God, but also the signs in the universe pointing to God's bounty.

Ayat al-birr   The "verse of mercy" (2.177), where it is claimed that Islam really consists of compassion and generosity toward the needy and is not the formalization of a religion.

Ayat al-kursi   The "Throne verse" (2.255), extolling praises of the majesty of God sitting on his "Throne".

Ayat al-nur   "The light verse" (24. 35), the most mystical Qur'anic verse referring to God as the "Light of Lights".

Ayat al-sayf   The "sword verse" (9.5), a very aggressive verse that urges the killing of idolaters wherever they are to be found.

Ayat al-umara'   The "power verse" (4.58–59), the most political verses in the Qur'an, urging those who wield power to use their authority with justice.

Din   Can be translated as "religion", but Islam is the *din* with respect to acts of worship and social activity, and also as an ideology and conception of the world.

Fatiha   "The Opening", the first sura of the Qur'an, particularly important since it constitutes the foundation of ritual prayer.

Fitna   A polysemic "word" meaning "disagreement", "hostility", "oppression". It is used in different contexts and has huge political implications both in Medieval and in contemporary discourse.

Fitra   The original conditions of humans in which God created everyone.

Hadd   "Limit" means both the "boundaries" established by God, which cannot be exceeded and are punished by penalties fixed in the Qur'an, and the last goal of human direction toward God.

Hadith   Usually translated as "tradition", but perhaps it is better to keep the Arabic term without translation: it means the reports and facts about the Prophet Muhammad transmitted first orally and then collected in writings in the ninth/third century. The collection of *hadith* form the *sunna*.

Hajj   The major pilgrimage to Mecca, which is obligatory once in the life of every Muslim who can undertake it (one of the five pillars of Islam).

Hanif   It could be translated as "monotheist". It is specifically applied to Abraham, who was neither a Jew nor a Christian, but "naturally" a Muslim.

Haqq   "Truth" or "reality" (contrasted with vanity and all error). Also one of the names of God.

I'jaz   The "inimitability" of the Qur'an, the miracle of its marvelous composition and its perfect order.

'Ilm   "Knowledge", the term used in the Qur'an to indicate religious wisdom or knowledge of God.

'Ilm al-makki wa al-madani   Knowledge of reconstructing and distinguishing between the verse and the chapters revealed respectively at Mecca and Medina.

Janna   One of the names, together with *firdaws*, with which the Qur'an refers to Paradise. Literally means "garden".

Jihad and Ijtihad   Terms that come from the verbal root *jhd*, which means "striving", "struggle" (on the path of God). *Jihad* is often wrongly translated as "holy war". Theologians distinguished between the "great" *jihad*, which is a matter of striving to regulate and improve behavior, and the "little" *jihad*, which is really warlike "struggle". *Ijtihad* means force in rational interpretation on the principles of law.

Jinn   "Demons". They are spirits created from fire; some are good and some evil, some Muslims and some unbelievers.

Mi'raj   The ascension to heaven of Prophet Muhammad, an experience that many Muslim mystics have tried (or claimed) to experience.

Muhkamat and Mutashabihat   Respectively, the "solid" and the "ambiguous" or "metaphorical" verses of the Qur'an. The former should be read literally; the latter, subjected to interpretation.

Mushaf   The Qur'an organized and edited "physically" in the form of a book.

Muslim   "Someone who surrenders to God", committing his or her trust and confidence.

Nabi   "Prophet". Different from *rasul*, this person is someone who is said to be called on to take on the role of personal warner in order to lead people on the right path. Tradition says there are 124,000 prophets.

Naskh   The science of abrogating and what is abrogated; it deals with which Qur'anic verses are to be abrogated and which replaced by other verses, based on their position in chronological sequence.

Qadar   "Power" or "decree" predestined by God.

Qur'an   The Qur'an in the sense of a book that is "recited". It is one of the many names of the sacred Book, among which are also "Book", "Scripture" or *Furqan* (that which discriminates).

Rasul   "Messenger", a type of prophet who brings a new Scripture, a new revelation. The principal messengers are said to be Adam, Noah, Abraham, Moses, Jesus and Muhammad.

Ridda   "Apostasy". The change of religion is condemned as a sin by the Qur'an, but no penalty is prescribed, at least on this earth, being the judgment exclusive to God.

Ruh   "Spirit". It comes down with the "Order" of God, *amr*. The Qur'an speaks of a "Spirit of Sanctity" and of a "Faithful Spirit", meaning the angels who come to bring revelation.

Salat   Ritual prayer, which is to be done five times a day at fixed hours (one of the five pillars of Islam).

Sawm   The fast from dawn to dusk during the sacred month of Ramadan (one of the five pillars of Islam).

Shahada   The profession of Islamic faith, first of the five pillars: "There is no god except God and Muhammad is the Messenger of God".

Sunna   The behavior of the Prophet, collected in the *hadith*. It constitutes, together with the Qur'an, the basis of *shari'a*, Islamic religious Law.

Sura   "Chapter" in the Qur'an; the Book contains 114 suras.

Tafsir   Traditional commentary, which in turn is either commentary according to the authority of the community and prophetic tradition that makes large use of the *hadith* or commentary according to the use of the intellect. It deals mainly with exterior, literary and historical issues.

Tafsir 'ilmi   "Scientific commentary", meaning to find in the Qur'an the foundations and revelation of all the sciences, especially the natural sciences.

Tahrif   Technical term that means "falsification" (literally, "changing the words") of Scripture as carried out by the Jews and Christians.

Tajwid   The art of recitation of the Qur'an, a distinguished profession within Islam.

Tanzil   Literally "descent", a term with which to indicate revelation.

Taqdir   God's determination that gives order and rationality to the universe.

Taqwa   "Piety", "reverence" and "fear of God". The best of humans are those who excel in piety.

Ta'wil   Commentary or interpretation of the sacred text in a very philosophical and/or symbolic style. It can be as much rationalist as gnostic/esoteric.

Wala'   "Friendship", the tie connecting all the believers who, as the Qur'an says, are "brothers". *Awliya'* are the "friends" and "helpers".

Wahy   "Inspiration", the channel through which the word of God was revealed to Muhammad.

Zahir and Batin   Respectively, the "exterior" aspect, literal and exoteric, and the "interior", allegorical and esoteric, of the Qur'anic text. Naturally, the *batin* has to be subjected to interpretation. They are also names of God.

Zakat   The ritual tithe, levied by the state to sustain the poor of the Islamic community (one of the five pillars of Islam).

Zina   "Adultery" or "fornication", considered a sin compromising the community's ethics and severely sanctioned in the Qur'an.

APPENDIX II

CONCISE TRADITIONAL CHRONOLOGY
OF THE REVELATION

Circa 570: birth of Muhammad during the so-called "Year of the Elephant" when an Ethiopian invading force against Mecca was dispersed by the intervention of God.

Circa 610: start of the revelation. The first suras to be revealed are 96 (Clot of Blood) or 74 (Turning of the Cloak). The Qur'an was revealed for the first time on the "night of destiny" between the twenty-sixth and the twenty-seventh of the month of Ramadan (97.1–3).

Circa 613: Muhammad receives the order to commence public preaching.

610 to 615: first period of the revelation or "first Meccan period". Within this period the following were revealed:

suras 81 (The Folding Up), 82 (The Splitting) and 84 (Splitting of the Heaven), the most efficacious in evoking the end of the world and the judgment of the living and the dead;

sura 53 (The Star), which contains a vibrant description of prophetic experience and contains the famous "Satanic verses";

sura 109 (The Rejectors), revealed to exclude all possible compromise between monotheism and Meccan idolatry;

sura 107 (Charity), which denounces the egoism and unbelief of the polytheists;

sura 1 or the "Opening" of the Book, which is fundamental for prayer;

sura 112, "Unity" or "Sincere Worship", which describes absolute monotheism—monotheism and eschatology are together with the appeal to social justice the fundamental principles of revelation during the first Meccan period.

615 to 619: the second period of revelation, or "second Meccan period". Revealed in this period were, among others, suras 18 (The Cave [much venerated]), 20 (Ta Ha) and 21 (Prophets), full of prophetic stories. Sura 36 (Ya Sin) is much venerated for its liturgical use during funerals. The abundance of revelations dealing with stories of prophecy seems to show that Muhammad acquired what was to be his own role in the prophetic history of revelation.

619: Starts the period of harder and more violent persecution by the Meccan polytheists against Muhammad and the Muslims.

619 to 622: the third period of revelation or the "third Meccan period". In this period was revealed, among others, sura 6 (The Cattle), one of the most beautiful and poetic of the entire Qur'an. Other important chapters revealed in this period of time were suras 30 (Byzantines [verse 30 contains the idea that Islam is very much a "natural" religion]) and 12 (which deals with the story of Joseph). The third Meccan period represents the phase of transition of major ethical, eschatological and theological preaching, and what one might call the more "political" aspects of the message.

622: the year of the Hijra or emigration from Mecca to Medina.

624 to 627: the Muslims fight against the Meccans, with varying success, three battles, that of Badr, Uhud and "the Ditch".

622 to 632: the "Medinan" period of revelation. Among the first suras revealed at Medina are the very long and complex sura 2 (The Cow), which contains all sorts of themes, from theological verses like that of "the Throne" (255), to verses with rules about pilgrimage

(196–200), to verses with prohibitions of usury (275–78), to verses that urge love and mercy (177), to verses that advocate war (190–93). The struggles and the battles fought by Muhammad against the Meccans find a resonance in the sacred text. The battle of Badr appears in sura 8 (Booty [especially in verses 5–18]), the battle of Uhud in sura 2 (for example 2.121–122) and the battle of "the Ditch" in sura 33 (33.9ff.). A chapter like 24 (Light) contains many mystical verses, like the very famous "Light" verse (35) and several normative verses (for example, 2–10, which deal with adultery). In the Medinan period, Muhammad is, to paraphrase Montgomery Watt, "prophet and statesman" at the same time.

628: the treaty of Hudaybiya sanctions a ten-year truce between the Muslims and Meccans.

630: Muhammad and the Muslims from Medina occupy Mecca and destroy the idols of the Kaʿba.

632, March: Muhammad makes his last pilgrimage, the farewell pilgrimage. Verse 5.3 was revealed, stating that the "descent" of the message was now finished and Islam is the definitive religion for humanity. Sura 110 (Triumph) is the last revelation of the Qurʾan and announces the triumph of Islam.

632, June: death of Muhammad.

APPENDIX III

WEBSITES ON THE QUR'AN

www.quran.org.uk is rich in Qur'anic texts and translations, and also has aural material on recitation.

www.midnet.co.uk/links/pages/quran has the text translated into seven languages.

www.quran.al-islam.com deals with the links between the Book and the fundamental principles of Islam.

WORKS CITED AND BIBLIOGRAPHY

MUHAMMAD AND HIS TIME

Armstrong, K. *Muhammad: A Biography of the Prophet*, Harper, San Francisco 1990.

Crone, P. *Meccan Trade and the Rise of Islam*, Princeton University Press, Princeton 1987.

Donner, F. *Muhammad and the Believers: At the Origins of Islam*, Harvard University Press, Cambridge, MA 2010.

Fitzpatrick, C. and Walker, A. (ed.), *Muhammad in History, Thought and Culture: An Encyclopedia of the Prophet of God*, ABC-Clio, Santa Barbara, CA 2014.

Ibn Ishaq/Ibn Hisham, *The Life of Muhammad*, translated by A. Guillaume, Oxford University Press, Oxford-London-New York 1967.

Lings, M. *Muhammad: His Life Based on the Earliest Sources*, Unwin, London 1983.

Rodinson, M. *Mahomet*, Seuil, Paris 1967.

Tabari, *Ta'rikh al-rusul wa al-muluk*. English selections, New York University Press, New York 1987 following (the volumes devoted to the life of the Prophet).

Vite antiche di Maometto, ed. M. Lecker and R. Tottoli, Mondadori, Milano 2007.

Watt, W.M. *Muhammad, Prophet and Statesman*, Oxford University Press, Oxford-London-New York 1974.

PRINCIPAL MODERN TRANSLATIONS INTO ITALIAN

Il Corano, a cura di A. Bausani, BUR Rizzoli, Milano 1988.

Il Corano, a cura di A. Ventura e I. Zilio Grandi, Mondadori, Milano 2012.

PRINCIPAL MODERN TRANSLATIONS INTO FRENCH

Le Coran, ed. R. Blachère, Maisonneuve, Paris 1951.
Le Coran, ed. D. Masson, Gallimard, Paris 1967.

PRINCIPAL MODERN TRANSLATIONS INTO ENGLISH

Al-Qur'an. A Contemporary Translation, by A. Ali, Princeton University Press, Princeton 1990.
The Holy Qur'an: Translation and Commentary, by A. Yusuf Ali, The Islamic Foundation, Leicester 1978.
The Koran, by N. Dawood, Penguin, Harmondsworth 1990.
The Koran Interpreted, by A. J. Arberry, Oxford University Press, Oxford 1964.
The Meanings of the Glorious Koran, by M. Pickthall, Dorset Press, New York n.d.
The Qur'an, by M. Abdel Haleem, Oxford University Press, Oxford-New York 2010.
The Qur'an, Translated with a Critical Re-arrangement of the Surahs, by R. Bell, Clark, Edinburgh 1937.

CLASSICAL AND REFERENCE WORKS

Blachère, R. *Introduction au Coran*, Maisonneuve, Paris 1977.
Burton, J. *The Collection of the Qur'an*, Cambridge University Press, Cambridge 1977.
Encyclopedie de l'Islam, Brill, Second Edition Leiden 1960- . . . (11 vol.). The third edition is in train to be published. . .
Goldziher, I. *Die Richtungen des islamischen Koranauslegung*, Brill, Leiden 1952.
Leaman, O. (ed.), *The Qur'an: An Encyclopedia*, Routledge, London-New York 2005.
McAuliffe, J.D. (ed.), *Encyclopaedia of the Quran*, Brill, Leiden 2001–2006 (6 vol.).
Nöldeke, T., Schwally, F. and Bergstrasser, G. *Geschichte des Qorans*, Leipzig 1909–1938, 3 vol.
Paret, R. *Der Koran: Kommentar und Konkordanz*, Stuttgart 1971.
Wansbrough, J. *Qur'anic Studies. Sources and Method of Scriptural Interpretation*, Oxford University Press, Oxford 1977.
Watt, W.M. and Bell, R. *Introduction to the Qur'an*, Edinburgh University Press, Edinburgh 1970.

RECENT WORKS ON THE TEXT
AND ITS INTERPRETATION

Abdel Haleem, M. *Understanding the Qur'an*, I.B. Tauris, London 1999.
Boullata, I. J. (ed.), *Literary Structure of Religious Meaning in the Qur'an*, Curzon, Richmond 2000.

Campanini, M. *The Qur'an: Modern Muslim Interpretations*, Routledge, London-New York 2011.

Cook, M. *The Qur'an. A very Short Introduction,* Oxford University Press, Oxford-New York 2000.

Cragg, K. *The Event of the Qur'an: Islam in Its Scripture*, Oneworld, Oxford 1994.

Cuypers, M. *Le Festin: Lecture de la sourate al-Ma'ida*, Lethellieux, Paris 2007.

Draz, M. *Introduction to the Qur'an*, Tauris, London-New York 2000.

Esack, F. *Qur'an: Liberation and Pluralism*, Oneworld, Oxford 1997.

Esack, F. *The Qur'an: A Short Introduction*, Oneworld, Oxford 2002.

Hawting, R. and Shareef, A. *Approaches to the Qur'an*, Routledge, London 1993.

Jomier, J. *Dieu et l'homme dans le Coran*, Cerf, Paris 1996.

Kermani, N. *Gott ist schön. Das ästhetische Erleben des Koran*, Beck, München 2000.

Madigan, D.A. *The Qur'an's Self-image*, Princeton University Press, Princeton 2001.

Merad, A. *L'Exégèse Coranique*, P.U.F., Paris 1998

Neuwirth, A. *Der Koran als Text des Spätantike*, Verlag Weltreligionen, Berlin 2010.

Neuwirth, A. Sinai, N. and Marx, M. (ed.), *The Qur'an in Context*, Brill, Leiden-Boston 2011.

Reynolds, G.S. (ed.), *The Qur'an in Its Historical Context*, Routledge, London-New York 2008.

Reynolds, G.S. (ed.), *New Perspectives on the Qur'an*, Routledge, London-New York 2012.

Rippin, A. (ed.), *Approaches to the History of the Interpretation of the Qur'an*, Clarendon Press, Oxford 1988.

Rippin, A. (ed.), *The Qur'an: Formative Interpretation*, Aldershot, Ashgate 1999.

Rippin, A. (ed.), *The Qur'an: Style and Contents*, Aldershot, Ashgate 2001.

Rippin, A. *The Qur'an and Its Interpretative Tradition,* Aldershot, Ashgate 2001.

Robinson, N. *Discovering the Qur'an: A Contemporary Approach to a Veiled Text*, SMC Press, London 2003.

Saeed, A. *Interpreting the Qur'an*, Routledge, London-New York 2006.

Saeed, A. *Reading the Qur'an in the Twenty-first Century: A Contextualist Approach*, Routledge, London-New York 2014.

Scarcia Amoretti, B. *Il Corano. Una lettura*, Carocci, Roma 2009.

Sharif, F. *A Guide to the Contents of the Qur'an,* Ithaca, Reading 1995.

Taji-Farouki, S. (ed.), *Modern Muslim Intellectuals and the Qur'an*, Oxford University Press and the Institute of Ismaili Studies, Oxford-New York-London 2004.

Wild, S. (ed.), *The Qur'an as Text*, Brill, Leiden 1996.

Zilio Grandi, I. *Il Corano e il male*, Einaudi, Torino 2003.

COMMENTARIES AND CONTEMPORARY
WORKS OF INTERPRETATION IN ARABIC

'Abd al-Hadi 'Abd al-Rahman, *Sulta al-nass: Qira'at fi tawzif al-nass al-dini (The power of the text: Readings on the utility of the religious text)*, Al-Markaz al-Thaqafi al-'Arabi, Beirut 1993.

'Abd al-Rahman Bint al-Shati', A. *Al-Tafsir al-bayani li'l-Qur'an al-Karim (Clear commentary of the noble Qur'an)*, Dar al-Ma'arif, Cairo 1968 (2 vol.).

'Abid al-Jabri, M. *Madkhal ilà al-Qur'an (Introduction to the Qur'an)*, Markaz Dirasat al-Wahda al-'Arabiyya, Beirut 2006.

'Abid al-Jabri, M. *Fahm al-Qur'an al-Karim (Understanding the Glorious Qur'an)*, Markaz Dirasat al-Wahda al-'Arabiyya, Beirut 2008.

Abu Zayd, N.H. *Naqd al-Khitab al-Dini (Critique of religious discourse)*, Dar al-Thaqafa al-Jadida, Cairo 1992.

Abu Zayd, N.H. *Mafhum al-nass (The concept of the text)*, Al-Markaz al-Thaqafi al-'Arabi, Beirut—Casablanca 2000.

al-Ghazali, M. *Nahw Tafsir Maudu'i li-suwar al-Qur'an al-Karim (Towards a Thematic Interpretation of the Qur'anic Suras)*, Dar al-Shuruq, Cairo 1995.

Ibn 'Ashur, M.T. *Tahrir al-ma'nà al-sadid wa tanwir al-'aql al-jadid fi'l-kitab al-majid (The explanation of the correct meaning and enlightenment of the new intellect in the glorius book)*, Dar al-Tunisiyya li'l-Nashr, Tunis 1979 (30 vol.).

Jawhari, T. *Al-Jawahir fi tafsir al-Qur'an al-Hakim (The pearls in the commentary of the wise Qur'an)*, Babi al-Halabi, Cairo 1340 H. (1921).

Khalafallah, M.A. *Al-Fann al-qasasi fi'l-Qur'an (The narrative art in the Qur'an)*, Maktabat al-Nahda al-Misriyya, Cairo 1950–1951.

al-Khuli, A. *Min hadi al-Qur'an (The guide of the Qur'an)*, Al-Hay'a al-Misriyya al-'Amma li'l-Kitab, Cairo 1978.

Qutb, S. *Fi Zilal al-Qur'an (In the shadow of the Qur'an)*, Dar al-Shuruq, Cairo-Beirut 1968 (8 vol.) [English translation by M.A. Salahi and A.A. Shamis, *In the Shade of the Qur'an*, The Islamic Foundation, Leicester 1999 . . .].

Rida, R. *Tafsir al-Qur'an al-Hakim (Commentary on the wise Qur'an)*, Matba'at al-Manar, Cairo s.d. (7 vol).

Shahrur, M. *al-Qur'an wa'l-Kitab. Qira'a Mu'asira (The Qur'an and the Scripture: Contemporary Reading)*, Dar al-Ahali, Damascus 1990.

Shahrur, M. *Al-Qasas al-Qur'ani. Qira'a Mu'asira (The Qur'anic Tale: Contemporary Reading)*, al-Saqi, Beirut-London 2010.

Shaltut, M. *Min hudà al-Qur'an (The right guide of the Qur'an)*, Dar al-Katib al-'Arabi, Cairo 1968.

INDEX